U.S. TRANSIT, TRANSPORTATION AND INFRASTRUCTURE:
CONSIDERATIONS AND DEVELOPMENTS

AMERICA'S MARINE HIGHWAYS

ELEMENTS AND BENEFITS OF WATERWAY TRANSPORTATION

U.S. TRANSIT, TRANSPORTATION AND INFRASTRUCTURE: CONSIDERATIONS AND DEVELOPMENTS

Additional books in this series can be found on Nova's website
under the Series tab.

Additional E-books in this series can be found on Nova's website
under the E-book tab.

U.S. TRANSIT, TRANSPORTATION AND INFRASTRUCTURE:
CONSIDERATIONS AND DEVELOPMENTS

AMERICA'S MARINE HIGHWAYS

ELEMENTS AND BENEFITS OF WATERWAY TRANSPORTATION

RAFAEL PELLETIER
EDITOR

New York

Copyright © 2013 by Nova Science Publishers, Inc.

All rights reserved. No part of this book may be reproduced, stored in a retrieval system or transmitted in any form or by any means: electronic, electrostatic, magnetic, tape, mechanical photocopying, recording or otherwise without the written permission of the Publisher.

For permission to use material from this book please contact us:
Telephone 631-231-7269; Fax 631-231-8175
Web Site: http://www.novapublishers.com

NOTICE TO THE READER

The Publisher has taken reasonable care in the preparation of this book, but makes no expressed or implied warranty of any kind and assumes no responsibility for any errors or omissions. No liability is assumed for incidental or consequential damages in connection with or arising out of information contained in this book. The Publisher shall not be liable for any special, consequential, or exemplary damages resulting, in whole or in part, from the readers' use of, or reliance upon, this material. Any parts of this book based on government reports are so indicated and copyright is claimed for those parts to the extent applicable to compilations of such works.

Independent verification should be sought for any data, advice or recommendations contained in this book. In addition, no responsibility is assumed by the publisher for any injury and/or damage to persons or property arising from any methods, products, instructions, ideas or otherwise contained in this publication.

This publication is designed to provide accurate and authoritative information with regard to the subject matter covered herein. It is sold with the clear understanding that the Publisher is not engaged in rendering legal or any other professional services. If legal or any other expert assistance is required, the services of a competent person should be sought. FROM A DECLARATION OF PARTICIPANTS JOINTLY ADOPTED BY A COMMITTEE OF THE AMERICAN BAR ASSOCIATION AND A COMMITTEE OF PUBLISHERS.

Additional color graphics may be available in the e-book version of this book.

Library of Congress Cataloging-in-Publication Data

ISBN: 978-1-62618-857-0

Published by Nova Science Publishers, Inc. † New York

CONTENTS

Preface   **vii**

Chapter 1   America's Marine Highway: Report to Congress   **1**
U.S. Department of Transportation,
Maritime Administration

Chapter 2   Can Marine Highways Deliver?   **99**
John Frittelli

Chapter 3   America's Marine Highway
Frequently Asked Questions   **117**
U.S. Department of Transportation,
Maritime Administration

Index   **121**

PREFACE

America's Marine Highway system accommodates the waterborne movement of passengers and non-bulk freight between origins and destinations otherwise served solely by roads and railways. Its corridors run parallel to many of the nation's most important land-based routes and connectors. These corridors are important components of the nation's broader domestic marine transportation system, which consists of 25,320 miles of navigable waterways, including rivers, bays, and channels, and many thousands of additional miles on the Great Lakes Saint Lawrence Seaway System and deep sea routes. For much of the early history of the United States, the network of waterways was the primary means of interstate commerce and transportation for goods and people. As a result, the majority of America's large metropolitan areas, as well as the preponderance of the U.S. population, are located along the coasts and navigable waterways. This book provides an overview of the current elements and benefits of water transportation, with a focus on a more environmentally sustainable transportation system; the marine highway and national defense; and impediments of new and expanded marine highway services.

Chapter 1 – This Report to Congress is required by Sections 1121 and 1123 of the Energy Independence and Security Act of 2007 (Energy Act). Section 1121 directs the Secretary of Transportation (Secretary) to establish a short sea transportation program and designate short sea transportation projects under the program to mitigate landside congestion. The Maritime Administration (MARAD) has implemented this short sea transportation program as the "America's Marine Highway Program" (the Program). The Program is intended to expand the use of our inland, Great Lakes Saint Lawrence Seaway System, intracoastal, and coastal waterways for the transportation of freight (loaded in containers and trailers) and passengers to mitigate landside congestion, reduce greenhouse gas emissions per ton-mile of freight moved, and accomplish other objectives.

The first section of this report provides the justification for expanding the utilization of Marine Highway services. It describes the interests of the Federal government in encouraging greater use of Marine Highways and, through the example of Europe, shows that government policy can be successful in achieving this result. An important point of this section is that the full range of public benefits of Marine Highway services will not be realized based solely on market-driven transportation choices.

The sections immediately following the introduction explain the potential contributions of America's Marine Highway to the following objectives:

- Improving our nation's economic competitiveness while creating and sustaining jobs, including through the reduction of landside traffic congestion, the ability to add cost-effective new freight and passenger transportation capacity, the reduction of wear-andtear on roads and bridges, and by providing resiliency to the surface transportation system;
- Providing an environmentally sustainable transportation system that requires less energy and reduces greenhouse gas (GHG) emissions per ton-mile of freight moved;
- Adding to the nation's strategic sealift resources and supporting the nation's shipbuilding industry; and
- Improving public safety and security through the safe movement of passengers and freight, including hazardous materials, and by enabling more effective transportation responses to natural and manmade disasters.

The report next summarizes the actions taken by the U.S. Department of Transportation (USDOT), through MARAD, to implement the short sea shipping provisions of the Energy Act. It begins by describing MARAD's rulemaking actions to implement the Energy Act, including the issuance of the Interim and Final Rules on the America's Marine Highway Program. Responding to the requirements of the Energy Act, the Secretary has designated 18 Marine Highway Corridors and has selected 8 Marine Highway Projects to operate on these corridors. Other actions directed by the Energy Act and undertaken by MARAD include efforts to promote the Marine Highway and include it in regional transportation plans; establishment of

Preface

agreements with other U.S. agencies to use Marine Highway services; consultation with shippers on methods to incentivize the use of Marine Highway services; establishment of an America's Marine Highway Advisory Board; initiation of Marine Highway-related research in consultation with the U. S. Environmental Protection Agency (EPA); and qualification of Marine Highway services to participate in the Capital Construction Funds program. This section of the report also highlights other important recent legislation by Congress, consisting of the National Defense Authorization Act for Fiscal Year 2010, the Consolidated Appropriations Act of 2010, and the American Recovery and Reinvestment Act of 2009, which established new grant authority and funding to support Marine Highway projects, including the recently-implemented Marine Highway Grants program. In September 2010, USDOT announced the award of grants to three Marine Highway Projects and funding for three research studies of potential Marine Highway services under this new grants program.

The next major component of the report summarizes other actions by MARAD to foster development of Marine Highway services. It cites the EPA's environmental leadership through its SmartWay program and its National Clean Diesel Campaign Clean Ports USA initiative. It describes MARAD's own efforts to promote sound environmental practices through the Environmental Achievement Program and the Marine Highway Benefits Calculator. The section also notes work with Canada and Mexico to promote Marine Highway systems for North America and MARAD's outreach efforts to the transportation industry and the public through its America's Marine Highway Program website. This section is followed by a description of important Marine Highway enterprises that MARAD has supported and includes a summary of the types of relevant business models for Marine Highway services.

The report proceeds to a discussion of impediments to the expansion of Marine Highway services, beginning with the needs such services have for specialized infrastructure and equipment. It notes the importance of reducing the costs of Marine Highway operations and administration through best practices and reducing the costs of transshipping cargoes through ports, making a case for government assistance to reduce the high acquisition costs for some types of specialized infrastructure and equipment. It also describes the importance of establishing reliable transportation services, suitable to just-in-time supply chains, as a means of overcoming shipper reluctance to try Marine Highway services. Finally, it cites the need to educate the public and transportation planners on the important role that Marine Highway services can have for improving public welfare.

The next to last section of the report identifies a range of potential legislation and regulatory actions that industry stakeholders have suggested to MARAD. These are actions, which are under consideration by the Administration and thus are not necessarily endorsed by MARAD, USDOT, or the Administration, that stakeholders say could induce increased waterborne freight traffic on America's Marine Highways. They include waiver of the Harbor Maintenance Tax for some non-bulk freight; equal Customs notification requirements for waterborne container shipments from Canada via the Great Lakes Saint Lawrence Seaway System relative to land-based shipments of the same containers; implementation of shipper tax credits linked to the value of public benefits associated with the decision to select water transportation; implementation of investment tax credits and accelerated depreciation for vessel and port equipment purchases; continued Congressional appropriations for matching capital grants such as those provided through the Marine Highway Grants program and, more broadly, the Transportation Investment Generating Economic Recovery (TIGER) and TIGER II Discretionary Grants programs (some of which benefited port-related projects); modification of MARAD's Title XI loan guarantee program to help introduce more environmentally sustainable vessels into the U.S. fleet; and establishment of a Marine Highway infrastructure-oriented program similar to the Transportation Infrastructure Finance and Innovation Act (TIFIA) program that could help to fund port and terminal intermodal infrastructure.

The report concludes with a section on conclusions. It cites the essential role that the private sector must play in making America's Marine Highway successful, but notes that without strong leadership from the Federal government the nation's water assets will continue to be underutilized for freight transportation.

Information in this report is current through December 2010.

Chapter 2 – Policymakers have been discussing the potential for shifting some freight traffic from roads to river and coastal waterways as a means of mitigating highway congestion. While waterways carry substantial amounts of bulk commodities (e.g., grain and coal), seldom are they used to transport containerized cargo (typically finished goods and manufactured parts) between points within the contiguous United States. Trucks, which carry most of this cargo, and railroads, which carry some of it in combination with trucks, offer much faster transit. Yet, at a time when many urban highways are congested, a parallel river or coastal waterway may be little used.

With passage of the Energy Independence and Security Act of 2007 (P.L. 110-140) and the National Defense Authorization Act for FY2010 (P.L. 111-84), Congress moved this idea forward by requiring the Department of Transportation (DOT) to identify waterways that could potentially serve as "marine highways" and providing grant funding for their development. DOT has selected several marine highways for grant funding totaling about $80 million. To be eligible, a marine highway must be an alternative to a congested highway or railroad and be financially viable in a reasonable time frame.

The prevailing perception is that coastal and river navigation is too slow to attract shippers that utilize trucks and that the additional cargo handling costs at ports negate any potential savings from using waterborne transport. While there are other significant obstacles as well, under highly specific circumstances, marine highways might attract truck freight. Freight corridors characterized by an imbalance in the directional flow of container equipment; shippers with low value, heavy cargoes, and waterside production facilities; and connections with coastal hub ports over medium distances may be suitable for container-on-barge (COB) or coastal shipping services. It also appears that marine highways are more suitable to international rather than domestic shippers because the former have lower service expectations.

A review of the successes and failures of the few marine highway services currently operating in the contiguous United States, as well as those that have failed in the past, indicates that the potential market is limited. In many instances, marine highways have succeeded in capturing only a negligible share of container shipments along a given route. One can question, therefore, whether marine highways will divert enough trucks to provide public benefits commensurate with their costs. Congress may also consider repealing a port use charge, the harbor maintenance tax, for containerized domestic shipments as a means of spurring marine highway development. Repealing the tax raises equity issues because waterway users already benefit from reduced federal user charges compared to trucks, and their other competitor, the railroads, are largely self-financed. The Jones Act is arguably another potential statutory hindrance to marine highway development, particularly coastal highways. This act requires that all domestic shipping be carried in U.S. built ships. Critics claim the act raises the cost of domestic shipping to such a degree that it cannot compete with truck and rail.

Chapter 3 – This is the America's Marine Highway Frequently Asked Questions, by U.S. Department of Transportation, Maritime Administration.

In: America's Marine Highways
Editor: Rafael Pelletier

ISBN: 978-1-62618-857-0
© 2013 Nova Science Publishers, Inc.

Chapter 1

AMERICA'S MARINE HIGHWAY: REPORT TO CONGRESS[*]

U.S. Department of Transportation, Maritime Administration

ABBREVIATIONS

BTS	Bureau of Transportation Statistics
BTU	British Thermal Unit
CBP	U.S. Customs and Border Protection
CCF	Capital Construction Fund
CMAQ	Congestion Mitigation and Air Quality
CNO	Chief of Naval Operations
CO2	Carbon dioxide
DOD	U.S. Department of Defense
Energy Act	Energy Independence and Security Act of 2007
EPA	U.S. Environmental Protection Agency
EU	European Union
FACA	Federal Advisory Committee Act
FHWA	Federal Highway Administration
FRA	Federal Railroad Administration

---

[*] This is an edited, reformatted and augmented version of the U.S. Department of Transportation, Maritime Administration, dated April 2011.

FY	Fiscal Year
GAO	Government Accountability Office
GHG	Greenhouse gas
Hazmat	Hazardous material
HMT	Harbor Maintenance Tax
HIS	Interstate Highway System
IMO	International Maritime Organization
ITS	Intelligent transportation system
LoLo	Lift-on/lift-off
MARAD	Maritime Administration
MMC	Merchant Mariner Credential
MPO	Metropolitan Planning Organization
MSP	Maritime Security Program
MTS	Marine Transportation System
MTSNAC	Marine Transportation System National Advisory Council
NDF	National Defense Features
NEPA	National Environmental Policy Act
NHS	National Highway System
NHTSA	National Highway Traffic Safety Administration
NOX	Nitrogen oxides
PM	Particulate matter
Pub.L.	Public Law
Recovery Act	American Recovery and Reinvestment Act of 2009
RITA	Research and Innovative Technology Administration
RoRo	Roll-on/roll-off
RRF	Ready Reserve Force
TEN-T	Trans-European Transport Network
TEU	Twenty-Foot Equivalent Unit
TIFIA	Transportation Infrastructure Finance and Innovation Act
TIGER	Grants for Transportation Investment Generating Economic Recovery
TIH	Toxic by Inhalation Hazards
Title XI	Federal Ship Financing Program
Ton-mile	Physical measure of freight transportation output, defined as one ton of freight shipped one mile
TSA	U.S. Transportation Security Administration
TWIC	Transportation Worker Identification Credential

U.S.C.	United States Code
USCG	U.S. Coast Guard
USDOE	U.S. Department of Energy
USDOT	U.S. Department of Transportation
VISA	Voluntary Intermodal Sealift Agreement

EXECUTIVE SUMMARY

This Report to Congress is required by Sections 1121 and 1123 of the Energy Independence and Security Act of 2007 (Energy Act). Section 1121 directs the Secretary of Transportation (Secretary) to establish a short sea transportation program and designate short sea transportation projects under the program to mitigate landside congestion. The Maritime Administration (MARAD) has implemented this short sea transportation program as the "America's Marine Highway Program" (the Program). The Program is intended to expand the use of our inland, Great Lakes Saint Lawrence Seaway System, intracoastal, and coastal waterways for the transportation of freight (loaded in containers and trailers) and passengers to mitigate landside congestion, reduce greenhouse gas emissions per ton-mile of freight moved, and accomplish other objectives.

The first section of this report provides the justification for expanding the utilization of Marine Highway services. It describes the interests of the Federal government in encouraging greater use of Marine Highways and, through the example of Europe, shows that government policy can be successful in achieving this result. An important point of this section is that the full range of public benefits of Marine Highway services will not be realized based solely on market-driven transportation choices.

The sections immediately following the introduction explain the potential contributions of America's Marine Highway to the following objectives:

- Improving our nation's economic competitiveness while creating and sustaining jobs, including through the reduction of landside traffic congestion, the ability to add cost-effective new freight and passenger transportation capacity, the reduction of wear-andtear on roads and bridges, and by providing resiliency to the surface transportation system;

4   U.S. Department of Transportation, Maritime Administration

- Providing an environmentally sustainable transportation system that requires less energy and reduces greenhouse gas (GHG) emissions per ton-mile of freight moved;[1]
- Adding to the nation's strategic sealift resources and supporting the nation's shipbuilding industry; and
- Improving public safety and security through the safe movement of passengers and freight, including hazardous materials, and by enabling more effective transportation responses to natural and manmade disasters.

The report next summarizes the actions taken by the U.S. Department of Transportation (USDOT), through MARAD, to implement the short sea shipping provisions of the Energy Act. It begins by describing MARAD's rulemaking actions to implement the Energy Act, including the issuance of the Interim and Final Rules on the America's Marine Highway Program. Responding to the requirements of the Energy Act, the Secretary has designated 18 Marine Highway Corridors and has selected 8 Marine Highway Projects to operate on these corridors. Other actions directed by the Energy Act and undertaken by MARAD include efforts to promote the Marine Highway and include it in regional transportation plans; establishment of agreements with other U.S. agencies to use Marine Highway services; consultation with shippers on methods to incentivize the use of Marine Highway services; establishment of an America's Marine Highway Advisory Board; initiation of Marine Highway-related research in consultation with the U. S. Environmental Protection Agency (EPA); and qualification of Marine Highway services to participate in the Capital Construction Funds program. This section of the report also highlights other important recent legislation by Congress, consisting of the National Defense Authorization Act for Fiscal Year 2010, the Consolidated Appropriations Act of 2010, and the American Recovery and Reinvestment Act of 2009, which established new grant authority and funding to support Marine Highway projects, including the recently-implemented Marine Highway Grants program. In September 2010, USDOT announced the award of grants to three Marine Highway Projects and funding for three research studies of potential Marine Highway services under this new grants program.

The next major component of the report summarizes other actions by MARAD to foster development of Marine Highway services. It cites the EPA's environmental leadership through its SmartWay program and its National Clean Diesel Campaign Clean Ports USA initiative. It describes

America's Marine Highway: Report to Congress

MARAD's own efforts to promote sound environmental practices through the Environmental Achievement Program and the Marine Highway Benefits Calculator. The section also notes work with Canada and Mexico to promote Marine Highway systems for North America and MARAD's outreach efforts to the transportation industry and the public through its America's Marine Highway Program website. This section is followed by a description of important Marine Highway enterprises that MARAD has supported and includes a summary of the types of relevant business models for Marine Highway services.

The report proceeds to a discussion of impediments to the expansion of Marine Highway services, beginning with the needs such services have for specialized infrastructure and equipment. It notes the importance of reducing the costs of Marine Highway operations and administration through best practices and reducing the costs of transshipping cargoes through ports, making a case for government assistance to reduce the high acquisition costs for some types of specialized infrastructure and equipment. It also describes the importance of establishing reliable transportation services, suitable to just-in-time supply chains, as a means of overcoming shipper reluctance to try Marine Highway services. Finally, it cites the need to educate the public and transportation planners on the important role that Marine Highway services can have for improving public welfare.

The next to last section of the report identifies a range of potential legislation and regulatory actions that industry stakeholders have suggested to MARAD. These are actions, which are under consideration by the Administration and thus are not necessarily endorsed by MARAD, USDOT, or the Administration, that stakeholders say could induce increased waterborne freight traffic on America's Marine Highways. They include waiver of the Harbor Maintenance Tax for some non-bulk freight; equal Customs notification requirements for waterborne container shipments from Canada via the Great Lakes Saint Lawrence Seaway System relative to land-based shipments of the same containers; implementation of shipper tax credits linked to the value of public benefits associated with the decision to select water transportation; implementation of investment tax credits and accelerated depreciation for vessel and port equipment purchases; continued Congressional appropriations for matching capital grants such as those provided through the Marine Highway Grants program and, more broadly, the Transportation Investment Generating Economic Recovery (TIGER) and TIGER II Discretionary Grants programs (some of which benefited port-related projects); modification of MARAD's Title XI loan guarantee program to help introduce more environmentally sustainable vessels into the U.S. fleet; and establishment of a Marine Highway infrastructure-oriented program similar to the Transportation Infrastructure Finance and Innovation Act (TIFIA) program that could help to fund port and terminal intermodal infrastructure.

The report concludes with a section on conclusions. It cites the essential role that the private sector must play in making America's Marine Highway successful, but notes that without strong leadership from the Federal government the nation's water assets will continue to be underutilized for freight transportation.

Information in this report is current through December 2010.

INTRODUCTION: AMERICA'S MARINE HIGHWAY

America's Marine Highway system accommodates the waterborne movement of passengers and non-bulk freight between origins and destinations otherwise served solely by roads and railways.[2] Its corridors run parallel to many of the nation's most important land-based routes and connectors.

These corridors are important components of the nation's broader domestic marine transportation system, which consists of 25,320 miles of navigable waterways, including rivers, bays, and channels, and many thousands of additional miles on the Great Lakes Saint Lawrence Seaway System and deep sea routes.

For much of the early history of the United States, the network of waterways was the primary means of interstate commerce and transportation for goods and people. As a result, the majority of America's large metropolitan areas, as well as the preponderance of the U.S. population, are located along the coasts and navigable waterways.

Over time, however, services along these waterways were first supplemented and then largely replaced by rail, road, and air transportation services as our principal means of movement.[3] In fact, while vessels on the U.S. inland river system, Great Lakes, intraport, and coastal areas still move more than one billion tons of freight each year, water services carried only 13 percent of the nation's ton-miles of domestic freight in 2007 – down from more than 26 percent in 1965.[4]

Inadequacy of Our Transportation System for Future Needs

It has become increasingly evident that the current system of freight transportation in the United States will be hard-pressed to meet the nation's future transportation needs with regard to maintaining national economic competitiveness, environmental sustainability, public safety, and emergency preparedness. Freight tonnage of all types, including exports, imports, and domestic shipments, is expected to grow 73 percent by 2035 from 2008 levels.[5] Land-based infrastructure expansion opportunities are limited in many critical bottleneck areas due to geography or very high right-of-way acquisition costs, particularly in urban areas where surface traffic congestion is the most severe. In many locations, existing infrastructure is suffering from overuse and will place growing demands on scarce public and private resources simply to sustain it. Accordingly, traffic congestion will almost certainly worsen significantly if the reliance on road and rail is not reduced.

The nation's heavy reliance on truck transportation for the movement of domestic freight (two-thirds of all domestic freight tonnage was moved by truck in 2008) has also contributed to the nation's dependence on petroleum.[6] Truck transportation uses significantly more fuel per ton-mile of freight moved than does water or rail. The U.S. Department of Energy (USDOE) reports that energy use by the transportation sector will continue to grow through the year 2035, and that freight trucks will account for the largest share (38 percent) of this growth.[7]

The nation is committed to curbing its GHG emissions, of which transportation is second only to electricity generation as a source. USDOE projects that GHG emissions from all transportation sources will increase by 195 million metric tons (10 percent) as of 2035 compared to 2008, of which 59 percent of the increase will be attributable to growth in heavy truck emissions.[8] However, some of the projected growth in both truck energy consumption and GHG emissions is likely to be curtailed through a regulatory initiative recently announced by the President. In particular, the President directed EPA and USDOT to take steps to reduce GHG emissions and fuel consumption by developing the first-ever GHG and fuel economy standards for medium- and heavy-duty trucks, in an announcement made on May 21, 2010.[9]

USDOT reports that approximately 5,000 fatalities per year were associated with heavy truck crashes over the last two decades (fatalities fell to just over 4,200 in 2008, however). Whereas USDOT, other agencies, and the industry are working hard to improve the safety of heavy vehicles, there are inherent dangers caused by the mixed operation of light and heavy vehicles in the same traffic streams. Our transportation system's current reliance on land-based transportation modes also creates potential safety problems involving the movement of hazardous materials through urban and residential areas. Although both water and land-based systems are vulnerable to major disruptions due to damage to key structures such as bridges and channels caused by natural or manmade disasters, the redundancy created by Marine Highways can help mitigate the disruptive impact of those events.

America's Marine Highway offers a cost-effective means to improve the economic efficiency, environmental sustainability, public safety and security, and resiliency of our transportation system. It also employs ships and mariners, providing jobs in peacetime and human and capital resources to deploy in time of war or natural disaster. Demand for ships to operate on Marine Highway corridors will also provide new business at the nation's commercial shipyards.

To date, the potential of America's Marine Highway to mitigate problems in the surface transportation system is not being met. As of December 2010, MARAD, which administers the America's Marine Highway program for USDOT, was monitoring only 32 Marine Highway and related domestic waterborne freight services that move containers and trailers. These and other marine transportation services moved approximately 2.05 million twenty-foot equivalent units (TEU) of loaded domestic containers and trailers[10] in 2008, of which just 11 percent (by weight) were moved in the contiguous domestic trades that compete with land-based transportation modes.[11] These 230,000 TEU compare to 3.85 million intermodal domestic rail container movements (consisting of containers and trailers ranging from 20 to 53 feet in length) in 2008;[12] highway domestic-only movements, which are difficult to measure accurately, would be much higher. USDOT believes that the full benefits of America's Marine Highway can only be realized if they are recognized, correctly valued, and facilitated within a comprehensive national freight strategy.

Why Federal Leadership is Needed to Develop America's Marine Highway

Our nation's current surface transportation system is largely the result of public and private sector responses to various economic and technological developments over the nation's history. It reflects the influences of changing industry and trade patterns, private and government investments, engineering and materials advances, the advent of new communications and computer technologies, and other developments. Driven largely by market forces, this system has provided the nation and the world with fast, affordable, and efficient transportation that has contributed greatly to the economic prosperity for our country.

Even so, our system is not as efficient as it could be. Americans using this system experience widespread traffic congestion, dependence on foreign-produced petroleum, high GHG and other emissions, high fatality and injury rates, and noise. Heavy vehicles operating on highways and bridges generate uncompensated infrastructure maintenance costs that all facility users and/or the public at large must bear. Marine Highway services have the potential to provide cost-effective, environmentally-friendly, safe, and resilient capacity that can mitigate many of these problems, but these services are only lightly utilized for the movement of commercial domestic freight or passengers. Given our nation's long-term and successful reliance on markets to steer resources to their best uses, the question must be asked as to why market forces have not led to more use of Marine Highway services.

Markets are optimal for allocating resources when the costs and benefits of an activity are well understood and factored into an investment or use decision such that the benefits of the activity are greater than its opportunity costs. Factors that affect market-based transportation decisions by private users of the transportation system include shipping costs, reliability and frequency of service, time in transportation, insurance costs, and quality of service. Other costs and benefits of our transportation system, however, are not borne by the private users who cause them. These costs and benefits are "external" to the user and typically will not influence transportation decisions made by the user. Common costs and benefits that are either fully or partially external to a transportation user's decisions include the effect that the user's decision to transport freight on a highway has on the delay experienced by all other users of that road, or certain effects that the choice of a transportation mode may have on jobs and the broader economy, the environment, public health and safety, and national security.[13] Unless such factors are addressed in comprehensive planning, investment, regulation, or market interventions, the full potential benefits of a transportation mode to both private users and the public at large may not be realized.

External benefits of America's Marine Highway that are often unrecognized in current transportation planning and investment decisions belong to the following categories:[14]

10   U.S. Department of Transportation, Maritime Administration

- Support for new and existing vessels and mariner jobs that are useful to the nation in times of both peace and national emergency;
- Immediate relief of surface transportation congestion, particularly on routes that provide landside access to urban ports;
- Abundant and cost-effective new freight capacity;
- Reductions in highway and bridge maintenance and repair costs;
- Creation of a diverse and more resilient transportation system;
- Improved environmental sustainability of the surface transportation system, including reduced per ton-mile energy consumption and emissions; and
- Benefits to public safety and security.

All of these benefits are in addition to the low-cost freight and passenger services that water transportation has historically provided and which are already considered in private decisions concerning the use of the Marine Highway. These external benefits are described in the sections of this report immediately following this introduction.

The correct valuation of such benefits in planning and investment decisions could justify a much greater role for America's Marine Highway as part of a balanced national transportation system. USDOT, with its responsibility to develop and implement national freight and passenger transportation strategies and target public resources to satisfy public needs across State and other jurisdictional lines, is best positioned to see that this role is realized. The Federal government is also well-situated to coordinate the development of national standards to ensure the compatibility of infrastructure and equipment throughout the Marine Highway system. MARAD is currently working closely with other USDOT modal administrations and the Office of the Secretary of Transportation to develop national transportation strategies that maximize the positive contributions of Marine Highway services.

National Support for Developing America's Marine Highway

Congress has understood the need to promote the expansion of the Marine Highway. In recent years, its most significant action in supporting America's Marine Highway was to enact the Energy Act. Among the many provisions of the Energy Act is Subtitle C of Title XI, titled "Marine Transportation," which requires the Secretary to "establish a short sea transportation program and designate short sea transportation projects to be conducted under the program to mitigate surface congestion."[15] The Energy Act recognizes environmental and transportation benefits of such services and calls for research in these areas. This would generate public benefits that include less delay and more reliable transportation as well as improved air quality, highway safety, and national security.

Congress recently passed additional legislation that will foster growth of Marine Highway services. This legislation includes the National Defense Authorization Act for Fiscal Year 2010 and the Consolidated Appropriations Act of 2010. The former act authorizes the newly established Marine Highway Grants program; the latter act appropriates up to $7 million in funds for the new grants program in Fiscal Year (FY) 2010. Additionally, the American Recovery and Reinvestment Act of 2009 created a discretionary surface transportation grants program in which Marine Highway port projects have competed successfully for grant awards along with highway, transit, and rail projects. The Consolidated Appropriations Act of 2010 created a successor to this discretionary surface transportation grants program for FY 2010.

The America's Marine Highway Program envisioned by USDOT will comply fully with Congress's legislative requirements for short sea shipping by working to bring about a more diverse, energy-efficient, and climate-friendly transportation system through the creation and expansion of domestic water transportation services. The goal of the Program is to develop and expand these services in a self-sustaining, commercially-viable manner that also recognizes the public benefits these services create in the form of reduced surface congestion, fewer GHG emissions resulting from a more sustainable transportation system, improved safety, and additional sealift resources for national defense.

The future success of Marine Highway services cannot be tied to any single factor, such as rising fuel prices or landside congestion. Rather, it is contingent on a broad range of qualities, none more important than the ability to serve the needs of shippers for reliable, innovative, and cost-effective transportation. MARAD is confident that the private U.S. maritime sector, with the backing of Federal, State, and local governments, will deliver the required quality and reliability of service needed to attract greater cargo volumes. The private U.S. maritime sector has expressed great interest in the Marine Highway initiative, including by its initiation of new Marine Highway services (discussed later in this document) and by providing extensive information to MARAD about the opportunities and impediments to such services. MARAD notes that innovation by the private U.S. maritime sector has directly or indirectly led to major advancements in international and

12 U.S. Department of Transportation, Maritime Administration

domestic shipping over the last 70 years, including the revolution in intermodal shipping via containerships, double-stack rail service (in cooperation with the U.S. railroad industry), improved logistics, new and larger ship types, and modern shipbuilding techniques.[16]

A full exposition of the Energy Act and other legislative requirements for the America's Marine Highway Program, along with USDOT's efforts through MARAD to implement them, is provided in detail in the latter half of this report. Information is also provided on MARAD's broader efforts to promote America's Marine Highway through support to local government planners and private sector water transportation services, as well as MARAD's efforts to identify impediments and solutions to impediments that will enable future growth of this national asset.

Effective Government Policies Can Work: European Union Example

There is good precedent for effective governmental action to support short sea shipping. The European Union (EU) is faced with many of the same issues as is the United States regarding surface transportation congestion, environmental impacts of transportation systems, and energy conservation. EU leadership has recognized that greater reliance on waterborne transportation is an important means of reaching its goals regarding environmental sustainability and economic competitiveness. It therefore has an active and longstanding policy of promoting short sea shipping and has invested millions of euros to promote greater use of its coastal and inland waterways, including:

- funding through the Trans-European Transport Network (TEN-T), the Marco Polo programs (designed to reduce congestion and improve the environmental performance of the intermodal transport system), the European Regional Development Fund, and State funding sources; and
- establishment of the Motorways of the Sea program (part of the TEN-T), the Program for the Promotion of Short Sea Shipping, and other and predecessor programs.[17]

As a result, container barge transportation has seen strong growth, with annual European traffic crossing the one million TEU level by 1991, the two million TEU level by 1996, and the three million TEU level by 2000.[18]

Estimated barge traffic in 2004 reached four million TEU.[19] Short sea shipping (here including bulk materials as well as non-bulk) currently represents 40 percent of intra-EU exchanges in terms of ton-kilometers.[20]

There are significant differences between freight transportation systems of Europe and the United States. Europe's rail system is less efficient than the U.S. rail system for moving freight, and Europe's geography has led to many of its largest industrial centers being in close proximity to water.[21] Nonetheless, the strong growth of short sea shipping of containers in Europe highlights both the ability of short sea shipping to compete with land-based transportation modes and the potential benefits of government support to this mode. MARAD is closely monitoring this successful European example.

IMPROVING OUR NATION'S ECONOMIC COMPETITIVENESS WHILE CREATING AND SUSTAINING JOBS

The efficiency of the surface transportation system underlies the efficiency of the entire national economy. As recently stated by the National Surface Transportation Policy and Revenue Study Commission:

> Transportation is the thread that knits the country together, providing the mobility that is such an important part of overall quality of life and is so deeply embedded in our culture and history. Highways, transit, rail, and water systems provide unprecedented access to jobs, recreation, education, health care, and the many other activities that sustain and enrich the lives of American families.[22]

The Federal Highway Administration (FHWA) of USDOT reports that the U.S. surface transportation system moved an average of 53 million tons of freight each day (including bulk movements on water) worth $36 billion in 2002, and estimates that by 2008 this freight tonnage had increased by 11.2 percent, reaching 58.9 million tons per day. Nearly 10 percent of this tonnage is imports and exports.[23] The surface transportation system also accommodated more than 13.6 billion passenger miles each day in 2007.[24]

Although the surface transportation system has handled traffic levels exceeding original design plans, demand for freight and passenger movement has grown more rapidly than capacity for the last several decades. The rapid growth in demand and the resulting capacity constraints became evident in parts of the U.S. freight transportation system during the 1990s and became a growing source of national concern particularly in the last decade. As noted recently by the Transportation Research Board, rising freight congestion threatens to impair economic productivity with the most visible congestion occurring at certain important nodes of the system and their surrounding areas, including the largest seaports and at terminal operations at inland hubs like Chicago.[25] Similarly, the issue of congestion for travelers on highways, transit, and rail systems has become severe in certain urban areas that are the major contributors to the nation's economic productivity. For commuters, traffic congestion can seriously impinge on quality of life.

America's Marine Highway is available to bring significant freight congestion relief along certain corridors. A study for USDOT estimated that there were a total of approximately 78.2 million trailer loads of highway and rail intermodal cargo that moved between origins and destinations 500 miles apart along the U.S. contiguous coasts in 2003.[26] This long-haul coastal truck and intermodal traffic accounted for 15 percent of total 527 million trailer loads of U.S. intercity truck and intermodal rail traffic in 2003. These movements do not include empty trailer movements or the container and trailer traffic moving on inland surface freight corridors that are also served by the U.S. inland waterway system. Moreover, they do not include potential freight on short-haul Marine Highway services.[27]

As will be discussed in more detail below, congestion at major ports can occur as freight volumes increase, as was demonstrated early in the last decade when some ports experienced double-digit year-on-year growth in international freight volumes. One benefit of expanding the Marine Highway system is that international containers could be transferred at major ports to and from Marine Highway services, bypassing the need to use congested urban landside access routes. Vessel operators serving purely domestic trades could bypass deep draft ports altogether, also reducing congestion at these ports. Most of the nation's smaller ports can handle substantial growth in container movements (subject to acquiring specialized equipment) with little or no congestion at the ports or on adjacent roads.

MARAD has not yet calculated the potential volume of Marine Highway movements of cargo through and around congested ports in U.S. markets, but such movements constitute a major share of the container traffic moved by water in Europe. Several recent startup U.S. Marine Highway services have or will specialize in the transshipment of international containers, including an Oakland to Stockton and West Sacramento, CA service and a Norfolk to

Richmond, VA service (see later report section on Other Progress – Marine Highway Services).

It is unlikely that Marine Highway services will offer a significant contribution to the long-distance movement of passengers within the United States given the relatively low speed of water service. However, passenger ferry services between or within highly congested cities can provide important relief to local traffic congestion and needed transportation redundancy for emergency situations. Urban areas account for the great majority of U.S. traffic congestion.

Jobs

America's Marine Highway can support the creation and sustainment of desirable jobs for Americans. These jobs are provided through direct employment in marine transportation services and shipbuilding, as well as other services that support marine transportation. Water transportation positions are beneficial to both workers and the nation. The Bureau of Labor Statistics (BLS) reports that earnings for water transportation positions are higher than most other occupations with similar educational requirements for entry-level positions.[28]

As of 2008, the nation's domestic and international water transportation industry supported approximately 65,200 direct jobs, with an additional 97,000 jobs in port-related activities and 104,500 jobs in shipbuilding and repair.[29] The water transportation industry generated some $36.1 billion in gross output in 2007, of which $10.7 billion was value added.[30] Many of the water transportation jobs exist in the inland waterway and coastal systems moving bulk products to our gateway ports.

Marine Highway services can take many forms, ranging from self-propelled vessels operating between coastal ports to tug-and-barge services serving ports along inland and coastal waterways, and can serve various freight markets and schedules. A typical tug-and-barge service carrying containers between ports offers employment opportunities for the vessel crew, stevedores, and terminal workers who facilitate the intermodal transfer of cargo to and from the barges. Such job growth may or may not substitute for jobs in other transportation modes, depending on the markets affected and the design of the service (see below).

The U.S. Coast Guard (USCG) is responsible for the credentialing of U.S. mariners. With certain exceptions, individuals employed on U.S.-flag merchant vessel of 100 gross tons or over must hold a valid Merchant Mariners Credential (MMC) issued by USCG.[31] The MMC is a form of identification and contains the qualifications that a mariner holds based on training, experience, and completion of necessary examinations. Beginning April 15, 2009, all mariners holding an active license, certificate of registry, Merchant Mariner Document (MMD), or MMC issued by USCG must also hold a valid Transportation Worker Identification Credential (TWIC) issued by the Transportation Security Administration (TSA).[32] The TWIC was established by Congress through the Maritime Transportation Security Act and is administered by TSA and USCG. TWICs are tamper-resistant biometric credentials that are issued to workers who require unescorted access to secure areas of ports, vessels, and outer continental shelf facilities, and to all credentialed merchant mariners.

Merchant mariners are critical to the national security and economic needs of the nation. In addition to their importance as human resources for the nation's transportation system, many play a vital role in for crewing ships during national emergencies and wartime situations (see section below on The Marine Highway and National Defense). Qualified mariners must be ready and available when a national emergency occurs – the time required to train new mariners would make it impractical to mobilize U.S. sealift in an emergency if mariners were not already on hand.

The United States is also well-positioned to meet the demand for new mariners. There are seven merchant marine academies in the United States that graduate over 700 ship officers and engineers annually.[33] Private operators, labor unions, and other associations also provide training. Over the last decade, at least 19 maritime high schools began operations in the United States.[34] In 2008, MARAD announced a new curriculum for these schools that will help prepare the next generation of high school graduates for maritime jobs.

Expanded use of Marine Highway services has the potential to generate orders for new vessels. These orders could help to revitalize the U.S. shipbuilding industry and support the nation's skilled shipyard labor base through the construction of self-propelled vessels specifically designed for container and trailer freight movement and passenger trades, such as roll-on/roll-off (RoRo) trailer ships and ferries (see section below on The Marine Highway and National Defense). The direct number of jobs created per vessel constructed would vary by vessel size and type. Building a larger self-propelled coastal ship to transport trailers and containers might generate up to 600 job years of direct labor at the shipyard[35] Indirect jobs (jobs at steel producers and other suppliers to the shipyard) and induced jobs (jobs supported in the general economy due to spending of workers' wages) would add significantly to the overall employment impact. Construction of Marine Highway vessels built to a standard design and in serial production runs would also reduce per vessel costs and could lead to more vessel orders and jobs over the longer term. Growth in Marine Highway activity will also support land-based job opportunities – such as short-haul truck drivers and logistical business positions at Marine Highway ports.

Job creation on vessels and in ports due to the growth of the America's Marine Highway system depends largely on the numbers and locations of Marine Highway corridors and services that eventually emerge, future growth of domestic freight movements, future funding of infrastructure in water- and land-based transportation modes, and the complex tradeoff of jobs among these modes as one modal system gains proportionately more traffic than another. Ultimately, however, the principal source of new employment from America's Marine Highway will be its contribution to the efficiency and flexibility of the nation's supply chain, as described in the following sections of this report. By having access to a reliable transportation alternative that can be expanded at modest cost when compared to surface transportation services, U.S. businesses can better react to changing supply chain circumstances, such as rising fuel costs, and thereby realize productivity gains and improved profitability. Profitable and productive businesses experiencing growth are the chief sources of new demand for workers throughout the economy.

Reducing Congestion on Our Surface Transportation Systems

Traffic congestion imposes serious costs on society in the form of time wasted in travel, fuel consumed and emissions generated in traffic backups, disruptions to supply chains, and major diminishments to the quality of life of the traveling public. Accordingly, efforts to reduce congestion have high potential payoffs to society, allowing greater national productivity through improved reliability of deliveries and trip times, lower transportation costs, cleaner air, and a much higher quality of life for commuters, persons shopping or running errands, family vacationers, and others.

Our land-based surface transportation systems are made up of a network of 4.03 million miles of public roads (8.46 million lane miles), 94,440 miles of Class 1 rail lines, 31,790 miles of combined Amtrak, commuter, heavy, and light rail passenger lines, and 1.69 million miles of gas and oil pipelines.[36]

Highway vehicles such as tractor-trailer trucks, buses and cars, and rail equipment such as freight trains and commuter trains, rely on these extensive networks to get passengers and cargo from place to place.

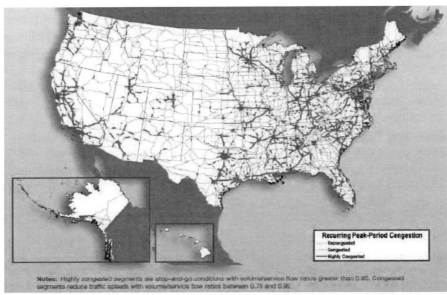

Source: U.S. Department of Transportation, Federal Highway Administration, Office of Freight Management and Operations, Freight Facts and Figures 2009, November 2009; Figure 3-10, p. 33. Note that the congestion map also corresponds to areas of greatest truck congestion.

Figure 1. Projected Peak-Period Congestion on the National Highway System: 2035.

As a general rule, if highway vehicle travel grows at a higher rate than road capacity, congestion will increase, and markedly so once the highway's design capacity has been exceeded. Between 1980 and 2003, rural and urban interstate lane miles increased by 17 percent, whereas ton-miles of freight moved by intercity trucks increased by 128 percent. Also during this period, the vehicle miles of automobiles (which share the roads with trucks) increased by 50 percent.[37] Accordingly, traffic congestion on the nation's roads has been increasing, leading to lost productivity from delay, greater unreliability in transportation services, and wasted fuel. The Texas Transportation Institute reports that the congestion "invoice" for the cost of extra time and fuel in 439 U.S. urban areas in 2007 amounted to $87.2 billion. Over that year, approximately 2.8 billion gallons of fuel were wasted and 4.2 billion commuter hours were lost to traffic gridlock.[38]

FHWA reports that 11 percent of the National Highway System (NHS) experienced recurring, peak-period congestion in 2002. It forecasts that by 2035 increasing truck and passenger vehicle traffic volumes will result in 40 percent of the NHS experiencing such congestion if there are no additions to highway network capacity (see Figure 1). This congestion will slow traffic on nearly 20,000 miles of the NHS and create stop-and-go conditions at times on an additional 45,000 miles.[39]

Rail networks are also not immune from congestion concerns. The past several decades have seen widespread concentration of rail services by Class I railroads, resulting in fewer miles of line operated. These fewer lines tend to have much denser rail traffic as carriers attempt to maximize the efficiency of their networks, increasing congestion. In areas where major rail networks intersect, such as in the Chicago region, congestion can be so severe that many shippers now plan for about a day just for a single train to traverse the city itself.[40] Travelers are negatively impacted as passenger trains share the same infrastructure networks as freight trains. As a consequence, some cross-country Amtrak passenger trains are consistently delayed.

America's Marine Highway can play a role in alleviating this congestion on some of our surface transportation corridors, with its abundant capacity to carry freight to and from many locations across the country. This is particularly true because many of the areas of greatest land-based congestion, as shown in Figure 1, are also those areas that Marine Highway operators could best serve through ocean, inland waterway, and lake access. While important at a national level, the Marine Highway can be especially effective in reducing congestion for all users along certain coastal surface corridors (e.g., the I-5 (Pacific), I-95 (Atlantic), and I-10 (Gulf) highway corridors), including at border crossings into Canada, and in urban areas with large ports.

The Government Accountability Office (GAO) has identified congestion around large urban ports as a major source of inefficiency in the national transportation system. The GAO notes the following:

> The major challenges to freight mobility share a common theme – congestion. National studies point to such problems as overcrowded highways and freight-specific 'chokepoints' that stifle effective intermodal transfer of cargoes. All 10 ports GAO studied faced similar congestion-related problems. For example, many of the ports are in dense

urban areas, limiting the ability to expand rail yards, roadways, and other infrastructure.[41]

The Marine Highway system has existing capacity to transfer containers and trailers away from congested highways and rail systems that serve ports to less congested ports and inland terminals. In 2000, FHWA estimated that each vehicle-mile traveled by trucks adds between $0.18 and $0.33 (reflecting typical or average conditions) to the cost of congestion on urban roadways; this value will only increase as congestion becomes more severe.[42] Reducing this source of congestion can therefore have significant value to the public. In addition to reducing surface congestion, the movement of cargo to inland terminals can benefit exporters and importers, many of which have found that their businesses are made easier if they can assemble export shipments or deploy imports at points free from the congestion.[43] Perhaps most importantly, it can offer shippers reliable and predictable service that is essential to just-in-time inventory systems. The America's Marine Highway Program is designed to identify the most promising water corridors for the movement of passengers and freight to help relieve surface congestion and to facilitate the transition to greater use of this underutilized national asset.

Cost-Effective Capacity Expansion

America's Marine Highway has many thousands of miles of uncongested capacity that can be easily accessed through many existing port facilities. Accordingly, it has the potential to generate new services and economic growth cost-effectively and in a relatively short period of time.

The cost-effectiveness of a specific Marine Highway service will vary according to the characteristics of the corridor it serves. For instance, existing shipping channels along the Atlantic Coast of the United States are already maintained to accommodate international trade and are more than adequate to handle vessels that would transport passengers and freight on America's Marine Highway. One study found that medium-sized, uncongested ports could be inexpensively modified to handle RoRo ships at an investment cost of $5 million each.[44] Moreover, many ports, including smaller ports, are currently capable of handling weekly, twice-weekly, or even daily RoRo vessel services, with ships that hold 100-150 trailers. The study further estimated that an investment of $50 million would be sufficient to prepare Atlantic Coast ports for liner loop service, consisting of vessel calls on ports in regular sequence.[45] The study notes that liner loop service would increase daily capacity along the Atlantic coast to a total of 21,000 trailers, consistent with the 10 percent market share projection common to several prior coastal shipping studies.

Marine Highway shipping along the U.S. east coast would directly supplement the I-95 corridor. The I-95 Corridor Coalition estimates that by 2040, miles traveled by all vehicles using the corridor will increase by 70 percent.[46] Truck volumes could nearly double even though such volumes are probably not physically or environmentally sustainable in many regions along the corridor. Further, ever-increasing congestion at highway and rail bottlenecks along the Atlantic Coast constrains interstate commerce and economic productivity. The Coalition estimates that to respond to this growth, approximately $47 billion per year would need to be invested along the I95 corridor on highways, $15 billion to $19 billion per year for transit, $4 billion to $5 billion per year for passenger rail, and $2 billion per year for freight rail. As noted above, the Marine Highway offers a relatively low-cost alternative at a public investment level as low as $50 million.

As noted, the cost-effectiveness of the Marine Highway investments will be service-specific and there are many freight corridors where water transportation is not an option due to geographical or other limitations. Nonetheless, where waterways are present, the incremental investment needed to accommodate passengers and freight on America's Marine Highway can be

22 U.S. Department of Transportation, Maritime Administration

very cost-competitive with existing land-based modes, even without accounting for the many other benefits provided by Marine Highway services.

Maintenance Cost Savings for Surface Infrastructure

Much of the wear and tear on our nation's road system is due to use by heavy trucks. The effect of truck weights on pavement and bridge maintenance costs is influenced by many factors such as vehicle gross weight, number and spacing of axles, pavement thickness and type, bridge type and span length, volume of truck traffic, numbers of overloaded trucks, effectiveness of enforcement of weight limits, etc. FHWA's Cost Allocation Study estimated that a five-axle combination truck with a gross vehicle weight of 80,000 pounds operating on urban interstate highways causes almost $0.41 in pavement damage per vehicle mile traveled (VMT) (this cost falls to less than $0.13 per VMT on rural interstates).[47] Adverse impacts can be greater, however, particularly for overloaded trucks that operate at gross vehicle weights exceeding 80,000 pounds.[48]

Research indicates that certain truck configurations can be used to minimize the additional damage caused by trucks heavier than 80,000 pounds on pavements. However, these trucks would still cause stresses that exceed bridge design levels and shorten bridge life. Building or strengthening bridges to accommodate trucks heavier than 80,000 pounds throughout the highway system would impose substantial, although as yet un-quantified, costs to the nation.[49]

Marine Highway services can accommodate the heaviest of containers and trailers without adverse impact to land-based or marine infrastructure, although in some cases terminal container yards and roads may require strengthening. Use of America's Marine Highway could therefore reduce lifecycle maintenance and replacement costs of surface infrastructure along selected corridors where heavy industrial or agricultural cargoes are carried. Actual impacts and savings would depend on the number of heavy and overweight cargoes transferred to water, enforcement of truck weight limits, the availability of drayage roads for overweight cargoes, the condition of the existing highway and bridges, and other factors.

Similarly, shippers using America's Marine Highway could benefit by realizing efficiencies of heavier container weights per shipment. In cases where cargo reaches the highway weight limits before the container's volume is completely utilized, shippers can find additional savings in the water option by utilizing all of the container's volume. For example, a shipper fitting 20 percent more cargo by weight into a container being shipped by water can experience an immediate and material savings on transportation costs. This is particularly attractive to U.S. exporters of the heavy industrial and agricultural commodities that will play an important role in the nation's economic recovery. America's Marine Highway may therefore offer a more competitive alternative for shippers of overweight and oversize cargoes.

Benefits of a More Balanced Freight Transportation System to the Economy

America's Marine Highway has an important role as an alternative and supplement to highway and rail movements of freight and passengers. An important component of the value of this role stems from its contribution to resiliency of the surface transportation system and in providing options to shippers and passengers who might otherwise be captive to another transportation mode. A Marine Highway corridor that is fully integrated with landside infrastructure can help to maintain critical interstate, regional, and local personnel and freight flows even in the case of multiple landside failures, such as downed bridges or flooded highways. The value of this resiliency to shippers and the economy at large is real and can be enormous when disasters and other blockages occur (see section of this report on Public Safety and Security). Even if such extreme events were not to occur, resiliency has a day-to-day value to the public. Economists attempt to measure day-to-day benefits of this resiliency through "option values." Water transportation services, such as passenger ferries, may have an option value to car-owners who value the opportunity to use the ferry service at those times when their vehicles are unavailable (due to breakdowns or weather), highway bridges become congested due to traffic incidents, or when they cannot drive (due to physical impairments). Thus, even though they may not use the water service frequently or at all, its availability has a real value to them. The same logic would be true, more broadly, for freight shippers and the nation at large with regard to the Marine Highway system. Although some shippers may choose not to use Marine Highway services, their availability during times of disruption to a preferred mode is of real value. Further research would be needed to quantify the option value of this system. In a more direct sense, America's Marine Highway offers real savings to shippers because it represents a competing transportation mode to rail and highway service.

Shippers who have access to more than one competitive long-distance modal service may experience lower shipping rates than do shippers who have access to only one suitable long-distance mode.[50] This is because a transportation provider is less likely to charge a rate premium when a customer can easily switch to a competitive mode. The value of having access to competing modes can be quite high even if one of the modes is less used than the other.

A MORE ENVIRONMENTALLY SUSTAINABLE TRANSPORTATION SYSTEM

America's Marine Highway offers the potential of significantly enhancing the environmental sustainability of the nation's transportation system. In particular, water transportation is often the most energy-efficient means of moving cargo between two points, with corresponding reductions per ton-mile in greenhouse gas (GHG) emissions. Similarly, with appropriate technology and regulation, water transportation is an environmentally-friendly transportation mode that can reduce noise and air pollution and have minimal impacts on water quality.

Energy Conservation – Reduced Reliance on Imported Oil

The U.S. Department of Energy projects that overall energy consumption by the U.S. transportation sector will continue to grow gradually for decades into the future, principally due to light- and heavy-duty highway vehicles (see Figures 2 and 3).[51] The highest growth in energy consumption as measured both in absolute and relative terms will be for heavy-duty highway vehicles, particularly freight trucks. Freight trucks are expected to account for 38 percent of the expected overall increase in energy consumption in the transportation sector by 2035, even though freight trucks currently account for less than 17 percent of total energy consumption in this sector.[52] When light-duty vehicles (e.g. cars and pickup trucks), commercial light trucks, buses, and freight trucks are counted collectively, growth in energy consumption in the highway sector will account for 78 percent of the 4.6 quadrillion BTU growth in transportation energy demand by 2035. This growth is expected to occur despite aggressive new standards established by the Energy Act of 35 miles per gallon average fuel economy for cars and light trucks. By 2035, the transportation sector is predicted to remain as the second-largest energy user in the nation after the electric power generation sector.[53] Further, the transportation sector is expected to continue to dominate petroleum and other liquid fuel consumption through 2035 (see Figure 2). There has long been recognition of the need to reduce our nation's reliance on fossil fuels as an energy source, particularly because this reliance exposes our economy to price shocks and supply disruptions caused by foreign geopolitical events. The Federal government has made important strides in improving the fuel economy of automobiles and light duty vehicles, and the President recently announced that USDOT/National Highway Traffic Safety Administration (NHTSA) and EPA will issue fuel efficiency and GHG emissions standards for commercial medium- and heavy-duty vehicles beginning with model year 2014.[54] Even with potential improvements in truck fuel efficiency, however, policies that encourage the use of freight transportation modes that are already several times more fuel efficient than trucking per unit of freight can help reduce our nation's overall energy consumption in the transportation sector. USDOT believes that the potential for modal shifts of domestic cargo from land-based transportation (particularly highway) to water currently exists in specific transportation markets and longer distance routes. An expanded or enhanced Marine Highway system could lead to more Marine Highway services being available to more shippers in more of these markets.

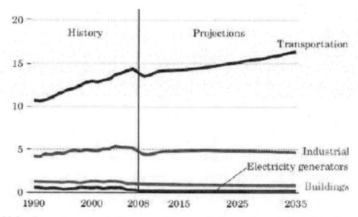

Source: U.S. Department of Energy, Energy Information Administration, Annual Energy Outlook 2010 With Projections to 2035, DOE/EIA-0383(20010), April 2010, Figure 79, p. 75.

Figure 2. Liquid fuels consumption by sector, 1990-2035 (million barrels per day).

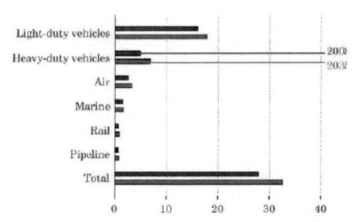

Source: U.S. Department of Energy, Energy Information Administration, Annual Energy Outlook 2010 With Projections to 2035, DOE/EIA-0383(2010), April 2010, Figure 55, p. 63.

Figure 3. Delivered energy consumption for transportation by mode, 2008 and 2035 (quadrillion Btu).

Research has measured the potential benefits of using more energy-efficient transportation services. One recent study found that while trucks, on average, can carry one ton of freight for approximately 155 miles on a gallon of diesel fuel (i.e., 155 ton-miles of freight per gallon, equivalent to 842 BTU per ton-mile[55]), rail achieves 413 ton-miles of freight per gallon (316 BTU per ton-mile), and a tug-and-barge operation can get as much as 576 ton-miles of freight to a gallon of fuel (227 BTU per ton-mile).[56] Additionally, self-propelled oceangoing vessels can have significant energy efficiencies over land-based modes, particularly in the case of larger vessel sizes.[57]

Not all studies agree in their estimates of modal fuel efficiencies.[58] Differences in fuel efficiency estimates among studies can be accounted for by numerous factors, including: when the study was conducted (engines are becoming more fuel efficient); haul distances and the availability of backhaul cargoes; the type of commodity being shipped (e.g., coal, grain, or other goods); ship size, hull shape, operating speed, engine type, fuel type, and capacity utilization; dependency on trucks for bringing cargoes to vessel or rail transfer points; assumptions about barge queuing and delays at inland waterway locks and ports; assumptions about bulk trainload and unit-train operations; assumptions about mixed freight carload traffic, trailer-on-flatcar, and container-onflatcar traffic; and other factors that will vary from market to market.

Collectively, however, research supports the inherent fuel efficiencies of marine transportation services. As such, shifting cargoes from pure long-distance land movements to water transportation in certain corridors would result in energy savings. These corridors include coastal corridors and those along inland waterways and the Great Lakes. Additional research, some sponsored by MARAD, will identify specific markets and routes within these corridors where shifting from land transportation to water transportation would yield the greatest potential energy savings. Water will not be the most energy-efficient means in all travel corridors, of course, particularly where routes are more circuitous or navigable waterways are not within reasonable proximity to shippers and significant drayage is required. Similarly, origin-todestination trucking can have energy-efficiency advantages over water and rail transportation, particularly for short haul freight movements where goods must be trucked to and from vessel and rail loading facilities. Fewer than 10 percent of large trucks typically travel to places more than 200 miles away, although these trucks account for 30 percent of the large truck mileage.[59]

Shifting cargo to more energy-efficient transportation modes could have important long-term social and economic benefits for our nation. Fuel efficiency, however, is but one of an array of considerations that affect the choice of shipping mode by private industry, and even here only indirectly through its impact on shipping costs. In many cases, the quality, convenience, frequency, speed, and reliability of a transportation service are critical factors in shippers' choices of a transportation mode that outweigh higher costs of a particular service attributable to higher fuel consumption. Accordingly, except under situations of extraordinarily high fuel prices that significantly increase shippers' costs, the broader range of national benefits associated with reducing fuel consumption by using water transportation will not be realized unless national policies promote the use of America's Marine Highway.[60]

Reduced Greenhouse Gas Emissions

There is a global recognition of the need to reduce the amount of GHG emissions released into the atmosphere as a result of human activities. Scientists are monitoring rising global temperatures and weather events, including droughts and more severe hurricanes, which are likely influenced by rising GHG emissions. The United States is second only to China as the world's leading producer of GHG, and within the United States, the transportation sector is second only to electricity generation as the source of GHG emissions (see Figure 4).

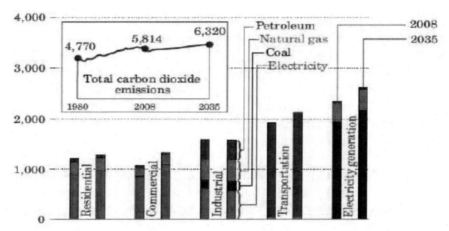

Source: U.S. Department of Energy, Energy Information Administration, Annual Energy Outlook 2010 With Projections to 2035, DOE/EIA-0383(2010), April 2010, Figure 93, p. 82.

Figure 4. Carbon dioxide emissions by sector and fuel, 2008 and 2035 (million metric tons).

Although significant reductions in GHG emissions per vehicle mile are expected from light duty vehicles (cars and light trucks) due to the mileage standards imposed by the Energy Act, USDOE projects that overall GHG emissions from all transportation sources will increase by 195 million metric tons as of 2035, or 10 percent, from 2008 levels. Approximately 116 million metric tons of this increase, or 59 percent, will be attributable to growth in heavy truck emissions.[61] These USDOE projections are subject to change, however. The Energy Act directs USDOT, acting through NHTSA, to develop a fuel efficiency improvement program and adopt a fuel economy standard for medium- and heavy-duty trucks.[62] Also, in May 2010, the President announced that USDOT/NHTSA and EPA will issue fuel efficiency and GHG emissions standards for commercial medium- and heavy-duty vehicles beginning with model year 2014. Accordingly, NHTSA recently issued a "Notice of Intent to Prepare an Environmental Impact Statement for New Medium- and Heavy-Duty Fuel Efficiency Improvement Program."[63] Because the rulemaking process is just beginning, it is too early to assess the impact this program will have on GHG emissions.

The greater use of water transportation could generally reduce emissions of carbon dioxide (CO_2), an important GHG, relative to other transportation modes. International Maritime Organization data reflect general values ranging from 117 grams up to 264 grams of CO_2 per ton-mile of freight for trucks, 15 grams up to 73 grams of CO_2 per ton-mile for U.S. railroads, and from less than 10 grams to up to 88 grams of CO_2 per ton-mile for self-propelled oceangoing ships.[64] In terms of the movement of containers and trailers, the range of CO_2 emissions for rail is likely to be from 51 grams up to 73 grams per ton-mile; for self-propelled ships the range would be from 53 grams (small containership) to 88 grams (small RoRo) per ton-mile. The use of larger self-propelled ships would likely lead to a lower range of CO_2 emissions. Many Marine Highway services, particularly those linking to the inland waterway system and along shorter coastal routes, will rely on tug-and-barge operations. A study by the Texas Transportation Institute calculates that tug-and-barge operations can carry freight at a carbon cost of as little as 17.5 grams of CO_2 per ton-mile.[65]

Future regulation of carbon emissions or monetization of their impacts would incentivize greater private use of and public support for Marine Highway services, but until such time, the benefits of water transportation, in terms of GHG emissions reductions, will not be reflected in comparative modal shipping rates.

Cleaner Air and Other Environmental Impacts

The expanded use of the America's Marine Highway offers other potential environmental benefits to the public. In addition to energy and carbon benefits, it removes freight traffic from land-based modes and thereby reduces the air pollution, noise, and vibration caused by heavy vehicles moving through urban and rural residential areas. In many cases, these benefits would improve the quality of life and livability of the affected neighborhoods. The actual impact depends, of course, on the extent to which Marine Highway services are used and a number of other factors.

Although water transportation is fuel efficient and produces comparatively small amounts of GHG per freight ton-mile, the issue of vessel emissions of air pollutants has been of particular interest in ports and coastal areas. Whereas standard tug-and-barge units burn highway grade diesel fuel, some coastal and most international shipping relies on the combustion of residual fuel oil (called

30   U.S. Department of Transportation, Maritime Administration

"bunker fuel") that contains high levels of sulfur and other impurities that contribute to regional and global pollution.

Fortunately, major progress has been made in recent years to reduce the environmental impact of vessel emissions. In May 2004, as part of the Clean Air Nonroad Diesel Rule, EPA implemented new requirements for nonroad diesel fuel that decreased the allowable levels of sulfur in fuel used in marine vessels by 99 percent compared to levels allowed before the effective date of 2007.[66] These fuel improvements, which went into effect in 2007, have created significant environmental and public health benefits by reducing particulate matter (PM) emissions from new and existing engines. In March 2008, EPA issued a final rule that implemented a three-part program that will greatly reduce emissions from marine diesel engines below 30 liters per cylinder displacement.[67] These engines include marine propulsion engines used on vessels from recreational and small fishing boats to towboats, tugboats and Great Lake freighters, and marine auxiliary engines ranging from small generator sets to large generator sets on oceangoing vessels. The rule will cut PM emissions from these engines by as much as 90 percent and mono-nitrogen oxides (NOx) emissions by as much as 80 percent when fully implemented.

Most recently, on December 22, 2009, EPA announced final emission standards under the Clean Air Act for new marine diesel engines with per-cylinder displacement at or above 30 liters (called Category 3 marine diesel engines) installed on U.S.-flag vessels. The final engine standards are equivalent to those adopted in the amendments to Annex VI to the International Convention for the Prevention of Pollution from Ships (a treaty called "MARPOL"). The emission standards apply in two stages: near-term standards for newly-built engines will apply beginning in 2011; and long-term standards requiring an 80 percent reduction in NOx will begin in 2016.[68] The requirements established in the rules will lead to much cleaner vessel operations.

The combined effects of the inherent fuel efficiency of water transportation and these regulations offer the potential for reductions in transportation emissions associated with freight movement. By facilitating Marine Highway services, States and Metropolitan Planning Organizations (MPOs) will be able to divert some surface traffic to water, helping to meet current and future air quality goals as well as reduce GHG emissions. The Marine Highway option will likely become more attractive to planners and the transportation industry as National Ambient Air Quality Standards are made more stringent as a result of periodic reviews. Notably, on January 7, 2010, EPA proposed the strictest health standards to date for ground level ozone (smog), which forms when emissions from industrial facilities, power plants, landfills and motor vehicles react in sunlight.[69] This proposal supersedes a previous EPA action to raise the threshold for air quality standards in March 2008, and will put additional pressure on some regions, including southern California, the Northeast and Gulf Coast, to undertake steps to reduce harmful air emissions.

The transfer of freight from trucks and railroads to the Marine Highway in urban areas can help to reduce the noise and vibration caused by heavy trucks and trains as they move through or past residential areas. Vessels typically operate along coastal areas and waterways with only minor noise and vibration impacts, removed by distance from residences and muffled because the vessels travel on water rather than highway pavements (Portland cement concrete and asphalt concrete) or rails. Simply reducing the number of trucks and trains can also improve the livability of communities by reducing public encounters with large freight vehicles on roadways and rail crossings. However, environmental impacts of freight operations in port communities will vary depending upon the local circumstances such as the percentage of freight transferred from vessels and carried by drayage vehicles and rail, the age of the truck and locomotive engines, whether port service equipment has emissions controls, the degree of congestion on highways in port communities, etc.

As discussed above, developing America's Marine Highway would produce environmental benefits in energy conservation and reduction of GHG emissions. At the same time, expanding the use of our nation's waters as "marine highways" for freight and passengers can also be expected to increase potential water-related environmental risks and consequences from marine transportation activities, operations, and accidents. Potential environmental issues associated with water transportation, if not managed carefully, include contributing to the spread of aquatic invasive species, increased erosion along waterways, impairment of aquatic habitats, and water pollution from fuel spills and other sources. Similarly, the construction and maintenance of waterways, in particular navigational dredging, can have adverse environmental effects, including impacts in downstream waters, wetlands, and estuaries. Increased water transportation could also affect the public's use of waters for recreation. As new Marine Highway projects develop, it will be important for private industry to reduce potential effects associated with discharges incidental to the normal operations of vessels, and ports should provide adequate waste handling facilities and management. It also will require continuing Federal leadership and broad-based coordination across the many departments and agencies with responsibilities in the U.S. Marine Transportation System.

32   U.S. Department of Transportation, Maritime Administration

Efforts to achieve this coordination will benefit the efficient and safe development of America's Marine Highway.

Accordingly, EPA, USCG, U.S. Army Corps of Engineers, MARAD, and other government agencies should continue to work with the maritime transportation industry to implement responsible regulations and practices to mitigate these potential environmental risks to our water resources. In addition to minimizing the occurrence of harmful events, a robust regulatory framework is appropriate to establish standards for sufficient contingency planning and adequate response resources for when such events do happen. Key issues to address include the potential consequences of the following:

- Future increases in water traffic and expanded infrastructure;
- Changed nature of vessels and their combined use and interaction on America's Marine Highway;
- Larger cargo capacities; and
- Changed and expanded cargoes and products and the nature and effects of accidental releases in multiple, varied aquatic environments (e.g., lakes, rivers, wetlands, estuaries, coastal ocean).

The full scope of these efforts is too broad to discuss in this report, and MARAD will conduct the appropriate analysis under the National Environmental Policy Act (NEPA) on both a project and programmatic level. Good environmental practice and sound regulation will be essential to achieving net benefits from greater use of America's Marine Highway on the nation's environment and quality of life.

THE MARINE HIGHWAY AND NATIONAL DEFENSE

Several aspects of America's Marine Highway are potentially beneficial to our national security. For example, certain vessels suitable for Marine Highway services, such as RoRos, could provide cost-effective military sealift capabilities at lower cost than alternatives such as procuring and maintaining comparable vessels in the government-owned fleet of cargo vessels. Even in the case of vessels not suited for military sealift, coastwise Marine Highway vessels would provide employment to trained officers and unlicensed seamen, many of whom could be available to crew government-owned sealift vessels in times of war or national emergency.[70] Finally, shipbuilding activities required

America's Marine Highway: Report to Congress

to produce and repair vessels to serve the Marine Highway can assist in maintaining this critical national defense manufacturing base.

Benefits to Sealift Capability and Resulting Cost Savings

To help ensure U.S. capability to project a global national security presence and sustain military operations abroad, the Department of Defense's (DOD) Chief of Naval Operations (CNO), in partnership with USDOT's Maritime Administrator, operates several programs to ensure sealift capability using a mix of government and commercial vessels.[71] The U.S. government fleet includes 49 government-owned Ready Reserve Force (RRF) cargo vessels, operated by MARAD and maintained in a readiness posture to allow them to put to sea in a matter of days. An additional 311 commercial U.S.-flag vessels in the Voluntary Intermodal Sealift Agreement (VISA) program are essentially on "retainer" for U.S. government emergency operations. The Maritime Administrator also administers the Maritime Security Program (MSP) which enrolls 60 modern, militarily-useful U.S.-flag commercial ships operating in the international trades to receive stipends and preference cargoes in exchange for access to their vessel capacity and global intermodal transportation logistics networks (MSP ships must also be enrolled in the VISA program). Collectively, U.S.-flag ships, in compliance with cargo preference law and under the leadership of the DOD's U.S. Transportation Command, have carried more than 90 percent of the U.S. military supplies destined for Middle East combat theatres,[72] including Iraq and Afghanistan.

The RRF vessels – and their crews – are a critical component of the U.S. Merchant Marine and regularly support defense and emergency response operations. During the first Gulf War, RRF ships carried nearly 700,000 tons of cargo on 123 voyages to the area of operations. Since then, the RRF has supported more than 400 additional operations and exercises for the DOD, including 267 missions for operations in Iraq and Afghanistan, and provided emergency relief for U.S. citizens in the wake of Hurricanes Katrina and Rita. Maintaining this sealift capability solely for these contingencies is costly, however, as large vessels must be procured, laid up in a non-revenue status, and maintained for long periods when not needed. The annual program cost for the 49 RRF ships was an estimated $277 million in FY 2009.[73] Moreover, many of the vessels in the RRF are nearing the end of their practical service life and must be replaced by newer ships. The estimated cost for this recapitalization for the entire RRF is in the billions of dollars.

Significant costs savings could potentially be realized by coordinating and planning the RRF recapitalization effort in conjunction with the development of high- or medium-speed RoRos for service on America's Marine Highway. To address this challenge, MARAD and CNO staffs are exploring a "dual use" ship concept that marries commercial capabilities and national defense features (see text box). National defense features include provisions for adequate range, speed, and specific cargo handling and communications capabilities beyond the needs of commercial vessels, but which are necessary to meet the needs of DOD during military mobilizations. These dual use vessels could contribute significantly to the America's Marine Highway mission, trigger much-needed business for U.S. shipbuilders, be largely self-supporting, and – when activated for emergency – support the nation's defense mission. The costs to the government of developing such vessels (including paying the cost of DOD requirements without commercial applications) could be less than those involved in the construction, lay-up, maintenance, and mobilization costs involved in building capacity solely for contingency operations. Careful analysis of the cost tradeoffs between using dual use vessels versus conventional RRF vessels for DOD sealift will be required as the dual use ship concept advances. Many of the vessels engaged in Marine Highway activities will not be militarily useful, particularly tug-and-barge units or smaller, shallow draft self-propelled vessels that might be used in the inland waterways.[74] Nonetheless, all Marine Highway vessels will employ U.S. mariners. The availability of trained and experienced mariners to crew RRF and other vessels in time of emergency has a high value to the nation, especially given the length of time it takes to train a new worker. Ninety percent of the RRF vessels have a nucleus crew of 10 mariners, kept available at a cost to the government. To operate, however, the RRF ships require full crew complements of nearly 30 highly skilled mariners. A robust Marine Highway fleet would provide an important source of mariners experienced at operating ships to meet sealift mobilization requirements. These mariners would not need to be supported at government expense but rather would be engaged in commercial activities until needed in times of national emergency.

Dual Use Vessel Options for Marine Highways and DOD Sealift Recapitalization

MARAD and DOD are exploring the concept of developing "dual use" vessels that can serve both the needs of military sealift capacity and the America's Marine Highway Program.

These vessels would need to be commercially viable for domestic U.S. east, west, and Gulf coast services while incorporating the National Defense Features (NDF) required by DOD in the event they are needed for military mobilization.

Fully implemented, the Dual Use program could help meet a limited portion of the military sealift capacity requirements. However, a sufficiently large Marine Highway fleet would have to be in service to allow labor and vessel capacity to be diverted to DOD service without causing serious commercial service disruptions. For example, if three to four vessels were in Marine Highway service in a given market, removal of more than one vessel for activation would most likely leave the remaining vessels unable to sustain the domestic service. Assuming a similar four-vessel service on each of the three coasts, no more than three vessels might be available for sealift capacity at any time.

To be commercially viable, the dual use vessels would need to be of moderate size and draft, capable of serving medium-size U.S. ports (a size that is also well-suited for ports in the developing world). Construction costs, which are typically higher in the United States than in many other countries, should be minimized by design standardization and series construction and perhaps Federal assistance. In addition, their operating expenses, crewing requirements, maintenance, and fuel consumption would need to be optimized for them to be financially sustainable in the low-margin U.S. commercial freight market.

NDF requirements might include specific speed and range requirements, cargo volume and weight needs, communications equipment, and self-loading/and unloading capability. Some or all of these capabilities might be accommodated most efficiently by designing in "foundations" for the equipment and, if called into DOD service, the vessels would be rapidly retrofitted by adding modules that provide the necessary attributes.

The vessels in general are envisioned to be RoRo ships around 600 feet in length and no greater than 30 foot draft, with a service speed of 18-22 knots. Exacting research and outreach is required to identify both the commercial attributes and the minimum NDF requirements of the dual use vessels, followed by initial design of a vessel intended for series construction. The costs of NDF requirements and NDF-related operating expenses are expected to be lower than the costs of otherwise sustaining defense sealift capability through conventional RRF vessel acquisition.

Maintaining National Shipbuilding Capabilities

The U.S. shipbuilding industry has long been considered strategically important to the nation, serving distinct military and commercial markets. Because the construction and procurement methods in these two markets are quite different, shipyards tend to specialize in building and repairing either military or commercial ships. The six largest U.S. shipyards perform the great majority of military work (almost 90 percent as of 2000) and do comparatively little commercial work (about 11 percent of the industry's commercial revenues as of 2000).[75] The more than 280 commercial shipyards in the United States have a strategic role in their ability to build and repair militarily-useful commercial vessels and can also be called upon to build and repair U.S. military vessels if the need arises. The commercial shipyards also produce large numbers of commercial vessels such as tugs, barges, and service boats that, while not militarily useful for sealift purposes, play an important role in sustaining commercial trade of the nation.

The order book for military vessels alone cannot sustain the U.S. industrial shipyard base. This is particularly true for the commercial shipyards, and there is growing concern about the ability of some of the six largest shipyards to survive on military orders. As pointed out by members of the shipbuilding industry, any lull in commercial vessel construction can adversely impact our national shipbuilding capabilities, as skilled workers are laid off and efficiencies and institutional knowledge gained during the production process are lost.

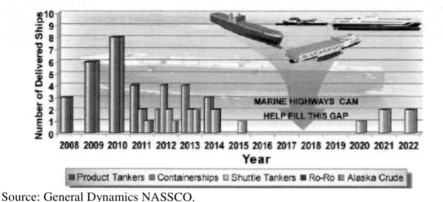

Source: General Dynamics NASSCO.

Figure 5. Projected Commercial Self-Propelled Shipbuilding Activity in U.S. Shipyards.

Construction of self-propelled Marine Highway vessels represents the potential for a substantial new market for U.S. shipyards, with some estimates ranging up to 30 vessels for long distance routes.[76] This new activity would be particularly important because a serious gap in commercial self-propelled vessel shipbuilding is forecast, which is illustrated in Figure 5. Vessel production for Marine Highway services could help fill this gap in production and contribute substantially to sustaining this important national industrial capacity. In addition, by establishing a more stable order book for new ships, shipyards will be in a better position to train and retain the skilled labor needed to lower productions costs and become more competitive. The jobs these orders would generate are needed by American workers as well. The Bureau of Labor Statistics reported that, as of 2009, national employment in shipbuilding had fallen by 3 percent since 2008.[77]

PUBLIC SAFETY AND SECURITY

Use of America's Marine Highway can improve public safety and security via several important mechanisms. By shifting freight from trucks on congested highways, the Marine Highway could lower the exposure of the public to the adverse effects of truck crashes. It is well-suited to the safe transportation of hazardous materials and reduces the need to transport these materials through population centers, thereby minimizing the risk to the public from releases of toxic cargoes. It also provides potential capacity in times of emergency for the provision of passenger transportation and freight service even after other surface movements are disrupted, facilitating response and recovery to both natural and manmade disasters.

Safe Movement of Passengers and Freight

Water transportation in the United States has established a sound record of safety for the movement of people. In 2005, U.S. ferryboat services provided 394 million passenger miles of service with no reported fatalities, up from 260 million passenger miles in 1995, again with no reported fatalities.[78] In fact, with the notable exception of the Staten Island Ferry incident in 2003 in which 11 people died, virtually no fatalities occurred on U.S. ferries over the last two decades.[79] Accordingly, the shifting of passengers from automobiles to ferry services, where practical, offers the prospect of safer commuter travel.

38   U.S. Department of Transportation, Maritime Administration

Associated fatality rates indicate that water transportation is also the safest means of moving freight cargo. In 2007, truck transportation accounted for 2,040 billion ton-miles of freight movement, with approximately 2.36 fatalities per billion ton-miles moved.[80] Rail transportation accounted for 1,819.6 billion ton-miles of freight movement in 2007, with approximately 0.47 fatalities per billion ton-miles moved (data collected from the industry by the Federal Railroad Administration indicate a lower rate of 0.33 fatalities per billion ton-miles of freight).[81] Water transportation moved 553.1 billion ton-miles of freight in 2007 with only 0.23 fatalities per billion ton-miles.[82] Actual safety improvements associated with shifting freight to water would be contingent on many factors related to location, drayage, type of cargo and equipment, and other items. The appropriate consideration of these factors can be assured through a robust regulatory framework with sufficient contingency planning and response resources.

Safe Movement of Hazardous Materials

The transportation of hazardous materials (hazmat) is naturally more complex than the movement of non-hazardous freight. The most hazardous of these materials are classified under Toxic by Inhalation Hazards (TIH). The safety, security, and liability issues surrounding the movement of these materials combine to encourage their transport by means that: a) provide the greatest separation between populations and the hazmat; and b) present the lowest risk of a release. While release of hazmat, especially TIH, is an infrequent occurrence, an incident can have very serious consequences. Not only does it endanger human lives, health, and the environment, it also has the potential to incapacitate critical transportation corridors or entire areas in the event of damage to infrastructure or forced evacuations.

America's Marine Highway offers several strengths in the carriage of TIH and other hazmat, including:

- An established safety record in the carriage of cargo that compares favorably with highway and rail;[83]
- Extensive experience in the movements of some bulk TIH products such as anhydrous ammonia and chlorine;
- The ability to carry hazardous cargo at sea or on rivers that typically provide significant separation from residences and businesses in the event of an accidental release;

America's Marine Highway: Report to Congress 39

- Little vulnerability to bridge or tunnel failures, including acts of sabotage targeting these structures; and
- Lower cost of transportation, including economic and societal costs.

The high potential costs of moving hazmat by land were clearly illustrated on July 18, 2001, when a CSX train derailed in Baltimore's Howard Street Tunnel causing a chemical tank car to rupture and catch fire. The blaze spread to adjacent rail cars and burned for five days, which the National Transportation Safety Board reported caused $12 million in response and cleanup costs.[84] The fire damaged infrastructure (including the street system above the tunnel) and shut down parts of the city. Additionally, the accident blocked the primary north-south rail corridor that serves the nation's I-95 freight corridor – a corridor that serves as a key route for the movement of hazmat, freight, and passengers. If this cargo had been moved along the Marine Highway corridor that runs adjacent to I-95, a release of this type, had it occurred, would likely have been much less disruptive to adjacent surface transportation systems. Other examples of hazmat incidents illustrate the danger and high potential cost of land transportation of hazmat cargo.[85]

As an alternative to land-based movement, water transportation of TIH and other hazmat materials could mitigate the risk of TIH releases, in large part by bypassing large cities and residential areas altogether. However, its full potential in this regard is not being met in part because many of the true costs of rail transportation of TIH are not borne by TIH shippers under current U.S. transportation policy. In 2007, 64 percent of TIH moved by rail, amounting to 105,000 rail-car shipments.[86] Not all of this carriage is voluntary on the part of rail carriers, however. Under Federal law, the railroads have common-carrier obligations to carry hazmat cargo and are limited in their ability to raise their rates to cover the costs of the risk (e.g., higher insurance costs) of carrying such cargoes.[87] As a result, shippers are able to move TIH cargo at rates that may be below the actual costs to railroads once the cost of insurance and risk are included.[88]

Marine Highway providers are not subject to the requirement to carry such cargoes and may not wish to offer services for TIH or hazmat products at rates competitive with those the railroads are required to offer. Ultimately, to move more hazardous cargoes safely on Marine Highway services, Federal action would be required to modify the common carriage obligations and rate regulation of the railroads to reflect more accurately the monetary risk and operating costs of moving such cargoes.[89] As noted earlier, significant policy determinations must be made to augment the economic viability of Marine

40   U.S. Department of Transportation, Maritime Administration

Highway services, potentially including policies related to cost-based pricing of hazmat transportation services.

There are certain caveats associated with expansion of water transportation of TIH and other hazmat products. Obviously, water transportation cannot serve sections of the country where waterways are not present. Marine vessels typically carry larger amounts of materials and, while in port, must be protected from acts of terrorism (this concern is greatest with regard to large international movements of dangerous cargoes into and out of urban ports).[90] Also, as greater use of water transportation of hazmat develops, increased training for first responders to spill sites must be provided. Plans and resources must be in place to ensure that there is sufficient capacity to respond to, contain, and clean up hazardous materials in the event that a spill occurs in a waterway or port.

Improved Response and Recovery

A transportation system that offers resiliency and affordable systems redundancy can assist in incident recovery and deter those who seek to do us harm. The value of this resiliency is augmented by the fact that water transportation is often not impacted by natural or manmade disasters, or if impacted, can frequently resume operations soon after the disabling event.[91] Also, as movable infrastructure assets, vessels can be relocated to provide assistance following emergencies.

The option to move freight and passengers by water as an alternative to land has proven critical to the ability of localities and regions to bounce back from several recent natural and manmade disasters. In each case, the Marine Highway and the vessels and mariners that serve on it played important roles in responding to and recovering from these incidents. The support of water transportation and its expansion could provide valuable response and recovery capability during future incidents. Several examples of recent, invaluable assistance provided by Marine Highway services are described below.

On October 17, 1989, the Loma Prieta Earthquake struck the San Francisco-Oakland metropolitan area, killing 63 people, injuring 3,757 and leaving as many as 12,000 people homeless. Both the San Francisco-Oakland Bay Bridge and the Bay Area Rapid Transit system were closed. That evening thousands of commuters, with no other way to evacuate the area, were delivered to the East Bay via ferry boats filled to capacity. More recently, on October 27, 2009 the San Francisco-Oakland Bay Bridge was closed to traffic due to the failure of steel support crossbeams that made the bridge unsafe for vehicular traffic. It was reopened on November 2. The closure again demonstrated the value of the Bay Area ferry boat systems. The systems saw a nearly 50 percent boost in ridership in four workdays of bridge closure, and in some instances ridership more than doubled.[92]

In 2005, when Hurricanes Katrina and Rita made landfall along the U.S. Gulf Coast, the Federal government quickly moved ten MARAD ships into the affected area to support recovery operations. The vessels provided food, shelter, and electrical power for oil refinery workers, oil spill response teams, and longshoremen who were essential to getting critical systems and supplies back on line. In all, these ships provided 269,000 meals and 83,165 berth nights for emergency relief workers and evacuees until the local infrastructure was repaired and available to support them.

Finally, and perhaps most dramatically, on September 11, 2001, with bridges, tunnels, and subways closed or disrupted, waterways offered one of the only methods of escape from lower Manhattan. An armada of more than 100 vessels, both public and private, was assembled to effect the largest waterborne evacuation since Dunkirk in 1940. In all, the waterborne evacuation of Manhattan transported as many as 500,000 people to safety. The ferry fleet was then used to transport emergency personnel and equipment to and from lower Manhattan, including military personnel and equipment (including tanks) to Governors Island and lower Manhattan.[93]

Not only do these examples demonstrate the potential for America's Marine Highway to help a region recover from an incident or disaster, but improving the redundancy of transportation systems can serve as a deterrent to terrorist attacks by limiting the duration and scale of intended disruptions.

INITIAL PROGRESS: DESCRIPTION OF ACTIVITIES CONDUCTED UNDER THE AMERICA'S MARINE HIGHWAY PROGRAM

While progress has been made to advance the concept of America's Marine Highway, much more work remains to achieve the expansion of Marine Highway services in our country. A modest number of Marine Highway services are currently active; MARAD is currently monitoring 32 regularly-scheduled domestic services that move containers and trailers by water (some of these services are to non-contiguous locations in the United

42   U.S. Department of Transportation, Maritime Administration

States). Many in the industry, however, point out that the concept of revitalizing short sea shipping has existed for well over a decade. In numerous conversations with industry officials, MARAD has observed a widely-held perception that Federal leadership is required to make further significant progress. Key legislation has recently coordinated efforts, established milestones, and funded activities to make notable progress. This section of the report will summarize MARAD's achievements in meeting legislative mandates as well as other initiatives currently underway to foster a vibrant industry of Marine Highway services.

Energy Act Mandates

The Energy Act directs the Secretary to "establish a short sea transportation program and designate short sea transportation projects to be conducted under the program to mitigate landside congestion."[94] The Act provides specific aspects of the program including agreements with other Federal entities to transport federally owned or generated cargo using a short sea transportation project;[95] an interagency board to identify and find solutions to impediments to the use of short sea transportation;[96] and research on short sea transportation.[97] Further, the Energy Act amends law to allow vessels engaged in Marine Highway operations to qualify for Capital Construction Fund benefits.[98] Sec. 1123 of the Energy Act requires the submission of this report to Congress. The full text of the applicable portion of the Energy Act is provided in the Appendix to this report. On October 8, 2008, USDOT issued a Final Rule in which the Secretary delegated to the Maritime Administrator the authority to "carry out the functions and exercise the authorities vested in the Secretary of Transportation" for short sea transportation, except the authority to designate short sea transportation routes and projects.[99] Accordingly, MARAD is identified in the following text as the responsible party for implementing most of the Energy Act's provisions.

Other Legislative Direction

Other recent legislation from Congress that will foster growth of Marine Highway services includes the National Defense Authorization Act for Fiscal Year 2010[100] and the Consolidated Appropriations Act of 2010.[101] The former act authorizes a new Marine Highway Grants program; the latter act appropriates up to $7 million in funds to the new program for FY 2010. Additionally, the American Recovery and Reinvestment Act of 2009 created a discretionary grants program of $1.5 billion for surface transportation infrastructure. Port projects, including projects serving Marine Highway services, were eligible to compete for these funds and received seven grant awards. The Consolidated Appropriations Act of 2010 created a follow-on discretionary grants program for surface infrastructure projects. More about these programs is provided in a later section of this report (see report section on Matching Capital Grants).[102]

Rulemaking Actions

The Energy Act called for the implementation of a number of rules and notices. MARAD issued an Interim Final Rule, "America's Marine Highway Program," on October 9, 2008, and amended it on October 31, 2008.[103] In addition to implementing the Program, this notice solicited comments on the structure of the Program and also sought recommendations for new Marine Highway Corridors. The Interim Final Rule established the goals and methods by which specific Marine Highway Corridors would be identified and designated by the Secretary; established the goals and methods by which specific Marine Highway Projects would be identified and designated by the Secretary; outlined how MARAD would identify potential incentives, seek solutions to impediments, and incorporate America's Marine Highway in State and local transportation planning; and described the research that MARAD, working with EPA, will conduct to support America's Marine Highway.

The comment period for the Interim Final Rule closed on February 6, 2009. After consideration and adjudication of all comments, MARAD issued a Final Rule on April 9, 2010.[104] The Final Rule adopts the Interim Final Rule, refines the definition of Marine Highway Corridors (and continues to solicit recommendations for Marine Highway Corridor recommendations), and establishes the eligibility requirements, criteria, and information necessary to apply for designation as a Marine Highway Project.

Corridor Designations

The Interim Final Rule (as amended) specified seven areas that public recommendations for Marine Highway Corridors should address. These areas

44 U.S. Department of Transportation, Maritime Administration

are as follows: (1) a physical description of the proposed Marine Highway Corridor; (2) the land transportation corridor served by the Marine Highway; (3) the organizational structure of the parties recommending the corridor designation; (4) the number of passengers and quantity of freight that are candidates for shifting from land routes to the proposed Marine Highway Corridor; (5) the potential reduction in surface congestion; (6) the environmental, energy, and safety benefits to the public; and (7) the anticipated impediments to establishing or growing the corridor along with strategies to deal with the impediments.

In response to the Interim Final Rule, MARAD received 59 corridor recommendations from public entities. MARAD reviewed the recommendations for completeness and compliance with the objectives of the Program. Some corridor recommendations were duplicative, and in many cases MARAD consolidated proposed corridors into larger units, ultimately leading to the identification of 18 all-water routes that can serve as extensions of the surface transportation system. These routes offer relief to landside corridors that suffer from traffic congestion, excessive air emissions or other environmental concerns, and other challenges.

The Secretary officially designated the 18 all-water routes as Marine Highway Corridors, Connectors, and Crossings on August 11, 2010. The 11 designated corridors are generally longer, multi-State routes. The four connectors represent shorter routes that serve as feeders to the larger corridors. The three designated crossings are short routes that transit harbors or waterways and offer alternatives to much longer or less convenient land routes between points. Collectively referred to as "Corridors," these 18 routes will integrate America's Marine Highway into the national transportation system and encourage the development of multi-jurisdictional coalitions to focus public and private efforts and investment. A map of the Corridors is provided in Figure 6. Note that the illustrated Corridors are generally located in those areas of the country that are expected to experience the most severe landside congestion in the future (see earlier Figure 1). More information about these Corridors is available at MARAD's America's Marine Highway website.[105]

Project Designations

In the Interim Final Rule, MARAD proposed an application process by which public agencies could submit water transportation projects for designation as Marine Highway Projects. [106] A Marine Highway Project is one that supports new or expanded container and trailer waterborne transportation services within a designated Marine Highway Corridor. The project must serve to provide public benefits along landside corridors in the form of measurable congestion relief, improved air quality, reduced energy consumption, infrastructure construction and maintenance savings, safety, security, and long-term economic viability.

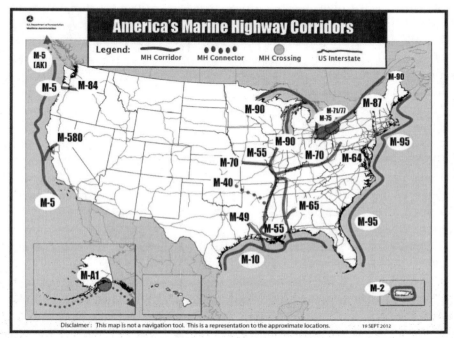

Source: U.S. Department of Transportation, Maritime Administration.

Figure 6. Map of Marine Highway Corridors.

Because Marine Highway Projects must be attached to a Marine Highway Corridor designated by the Secretary, and because such corridors had not been designated as the time of the Interim Final Rule, MARAD was unable to solicit the submission of Marine Highway Projects through the Interim Final Rule. Following the issuance of the Interim Final Rule, however, MARAD refined the Marine Highway Project application process and developed the procedures and other tools needed to process, review, and evaluate these projects once they could be submitted. MARAD designed the evaluation process to enable the selection of those projects which generate the greatest

46 U.S. Department of Transportation, Maritime Administration

public benefits and are most likely to support self-sustaining services in the next three to five years. The Final Rule for the America's Marine Highway Program contains information about the final project evaluation process.

On April 15, 2010, MARAD issued a formal call for Marine Highway Project applications by public agencies.[107] State Departments of Transportation, ports, and local transportation planning agencies from across the country submitted 35 applications to MARAD. On August 11, 2010, the Secretary selected eight projects from these applications for designation as Marine Highway Projects under the Program.[108] These projects, which serve the north, middle, and south Atlantic coasts, the Gulf coast, inland Mississippi and Alabama, and Michigan, represent new or expanded Marine Highway services that offer promise of public benefit and long-term sustainability without future Federal operational support. They will receive preferential treatment for Federal assistance from USDOT and MARAD. For instance, sponsors of designated Marine Highway Projects are eligible to apply for grants under the new Marine Highway Grants program, officially implemented by MARAD through a Notice of Funding Availability published in the Federal Register on August 11, 2010.[109] On September 20, 2010, the Secretary announced the award of grants to three Marine Highway Projects and funding for three research studies of potential Marine Highway services, totaling $7 million in funds.[110]

In addition to designating Marine Highway Projects, the Secretary on August 11, 2010, selected six applications as "Marine Highway Initiatives." These Initiatives, while not developed to the point of proposing specific services and routes required for Project designation, offer particular promise for the future.

They will receive support from USDOT and MARAD in the form of assistance in further developing the concepts through conduct of research, market analysis, and other efforts to identify the opportunities they may present. More information about the Marine Highway Projects and Initiatives is available at MARAD's America's Marine Highway website.[111]

Promotion and Coordination of America's Marine Highway

The Energy Act authorizes the Secretary to promote and support the development of America's Marine Highway.[112] Accordingly, for designated Marine Highway Corridors, MARAD will coordinate among Federal, State, and local government agencies to gain access to facilities and cargoes, support data collection and dissemination, conduct research, and encourage and participate in planning activities.

Similarly, MARAD will actively support designated Marine Highway Projects through technical assistance, grants (subject to funding availability), coordination, and promotion. It will also work with other USDOT operating administrations to identify existing and potential Federal, State, and local funding mechanisms to support these projects. Much more about MARAD's efforts to promote Marine Highways is provided in the later sections of this report.

Multistate, State, and Regional Transportation Planning

The Energy Act requires the Secretary to develop strategies to encourage the use of America's Marine Highway in State and local transportation planning.[113] MARAD has successfully worked with two east coast MPOs to incorporate and support Marine Highway services in their long range transportation plans.

Other new services developed by the private sector in cooperation with State and local planning organizations and MARAD will soon follow (see the section below on Other Progress – Marine Highway Services).

Memorandums of Agreement

The Energy Act authorizes the Secretary to enter into memorandums of agreement with the heads of other Federal agencies to transport Federal cargo using services supported under designated Marine Highway Projects.[114] MARAD has begun dialogues with agencies, including the Department of Defense and the State Department, to prepare for future agreements to move domestic freight, as well as to support existing services. MARAD expects progress in acquiring government domestic cargoes to be only gradual until Marine Highway service providers can establish a broad, integrated transportation network.

The State Department began using an existing Marine Highway service to ship government cargoes from Texas to Florida beginning in January 2009.

48   U.S. Department of Transportation, Maritime Administration

Short Term Incentives

The Energy Act authorizes the Secretary to consult with shippers and other transportation logistics stakeholders to develop proposals for short-term incentives to encourage the use of America's Marine Highway.[115] MARAD has consulted with stakeholders across the spectrum of the industry, including shippers and land transportation service providers, vessel owners and operators, and shoreside infrastructure owners and operators to assemble a series of potential short-term incentives. These incentives are described in a later section of this report (see Potential Legislative Actions to Support America's Marine Highway). USDOT is also prepared to brief Congress and provide more information on these incentives upon request.

Advisory Board

The Energy Act directs the Secretary establish a board to identify and seek solutions to impediments hindering effective use of short sea transportation.[116] The legislation requires that the board include representatives of EPA and other Federal agencies, State and local government entities, and private sector entities. MARAD will also include subject matter experts deemed necessary to a particular issue. This requirement was not, however, accompanied by any additional funding or staff positions.

After determining that the new advisory board must comply with the Federal Advisory Committee Act (FACA), MARAD explored the option of establishing the board within the framework of the Marine Transportation System National Advisory Council (MTSNAC), which operates under FACA. MTSNAC was chartered in 2000 to advise the Secretary, via the Maritime Administrator, on matters relating to the Marine Transportation System (MTS), waterways, ports, and intermodal connections. The MTSNAC charter expired on January 5, 2010. USDOT has reestablished a new charter under which MTSNAC will be able to accommodate both the requirements of the America's Marine Highway advisory board and leverage the expertise and advice of an organization designed to accomplish the original MTSNAC mandate.

The re-established MTSNAC will remain advisory in nature and will not develop regulations, formulate policy, create incentives, or determine Federal budget priorities. The Council will, however, identify and recommend solutions to impediments or barriers to the expansion, development, and effective use of America's Marine Highway.

It will also provide advice and recommendations concerning waterways, ports, and intermodal connectors, as well as MTS issues regarding the environment, safety, livable communities, global competitiveness, national security, and MTS performance. These objectives will parallel those of the previous MTSNAC.

Marine Highway Research

The Energy Act authorizes the Secretary to conduct Marine Highway-related research in consultation with the Administrator of the EPA and other public and private entities.[117]

Research can include identification of existing or emerging technology, vessel design, and other improvements that would reduce emissions, increase fuel economy, lower costs, and improve efficiency of Marine Highway transportation. While no Federal funds have been specifically appropriated for Marine Highway research, research activities are being conducted through various mechanisms described in the next section of the report (see Additional Actions for America's Marine Highway).

MARAD has developed several research proposals that could yield information valuable to the near- and long-term expansion of Marine Highway services.

Each of these proposals can be implemented quickly and completed within one to two years following the identification of funding sources. The costs of each study would vary, ranging from $100,000 to over $1,000,000 if technology deployment is required.

- Quantification of Public Benefits – Quantify the net present value of external cost savings and other public benefits that could be derived from one or more specific, regional marine highway services in the United States. The analysis would quantify the monetized values of Marine Highway service contributions to landside congestion savings, emissions and energy use reductions, landside transportation infrastructure maintenance savings, safety improvements, improved resiliency, and reduced costs of national sealift. Specific conditions of regional markets could be studied and projected over a 20+ year project life.

50   U.S. Department of Transportation, Maritime Administration

- Vessel Design Research – In cooperation with industry and other government agencies, identify optimal Marine Highway vessel designs for inland, coastal, and intracoastal trade routes. The study would consider various RoRo, containership, and other designs to provide efficient intermodal transfers to reduce cargo transit time, cost, and environmental impacts. This effort would evaluate the commercial and sealift effects of the potential inclusion of National Defense Features. MARAD has initiated a design study, and expects to obtain results in 2011.
- Intermodal Transfer (Terminal Design) – Develop a set of Marine Highway optimal terminal configuration guidelines to facilitate the intermodal transfer of goods in containers and trailers between Marine Highway services and landside transportation modes; and marine/intermodal terminals and inland, intracoastal and coastal vessels. The goal of the research is to reduce transfer time and costs and to better integrate Marine Highway services into the national transportation network. This study must be conducted in concert with the vessel design research described immediately above to insure that maximum cargo handling efficiencies can be realized.
- Maritime Intelligent Transportation System (ITS) Applications – Investigate the range of ITS applications that can provide greater operational efficiencies within the Marine Highway service environment. The latter part of the research effort would focus on deploying selected pilot projects. The research would establish a baseline for ITS service and determine potential efficiencies and cost savings.

Capital Construction Fund

The Energy Act modifies certain statutes to allow container-carrying and RoRo vessels engaged in Marine Highway operations to qualify for Capital Construction Fund (CCF) benefits.[118] The CCF encourages construction, reconstruction, or acquisition of vessels through the deferment of Federal income taxes on certain deposits of money or other property placed into a CCF account. MARAD has completed all of the necessary actions to implement this section of the Energy Act, which is now in effect.

ADDITIONAL ACTIONS FOR AMERICA'S MARINE HIGHWAY

In keeping with the clear direction from the Energy Act that it should promote and coordinate the development of America's Marine Highway, USDOT is engaged in numerous activities in addition to those specifically required by the Energy Act to accomplish this mandate. The most important of these activities are described in this report section.

Environmental Leadership

MARAD is working in partnership with EPA to provide incentives for shippers and Marine Highway service providers to consider environmental factors when planning their freight moves. MARAD will also formally involve EPA in the new America's Marine Highway Advisory Board.

Environmental Protection Agency Partnership

MARAD is supporting EPA's SmartWay Transport Partnership Program. SmartWay Transport is an innovative collaboration between EPA and the nation's freight sector to improve energy efficiency, reduce GHG and air pollutant emissions, and improve energy security. Companies that participate in SmartWay Transport programs save money, reduce fuel consumption, and are recognized for their social responsibility and leadership.

EPA is currently working with its shipper partners, leaders in the shipping industry, and MARAD to explore the potential to integrate a maritime component into SmartWay Transport and identify GHG emissions-reduction and fuel-conservation strategies for Marine Highway vessels. SmartWay Transport will serve as an excellent catalyst for companies to explore and support the opportunities that the America's Marine Highway Program offers for cost-effective and environmentally friendly freight transportation. Ultimately, this program will offer a valuable means to measurably reduce carbon emissions by choosing Marine Highway services. Additionally, EPA's National Clean Diesel Campaign is working through its Clean Ports USA initiative to reduce harmful diesel emissions from ports by retrofitting, replacing, repowering, or refueling older diesel engines in port equipment and vessels.[119]

52 U.S. Department of Transportation, Maritime Administration

Environmental Achievement Program

In an effort to provide increased environmental incentives for Marine Highway projects, MARAD has contracted with the University of Delaware to conduct an environmental benchmarks study.

The results of this study will identify a group of practical activities that Marine Highway operators can undertake to exceed minimal compliance with laws and regulations on environmental quality.

This study will become the foundation for an environmental achievement program to recognize operators for their implementation of best practices in services and terminal activities. This program is being coordinated with EPA to ensure consistent Federal policy and promote shared objectives. Likely activities that would receive recognition are the use of ultra low sulfur fuels by Marine Highway vessels, low VOC (volatile organic compounds) paints on vessel hulls, use of low-impact lubricants, crew awareness training, responsible water and ballast discharge protocols, and use of new fuel efficiency, energy conservation, and emissions reduction technologies and operational practices.

Enabling Transportation Funding – Marine Highway Benefits (Emissions Reduction) Calculator

State and local transportation planners, especially in air quality "nonattainment" areas, are required to invest certain funds in ways that reduce surface congestion and improve air quality.[120]

Some State and local transportation planners, however, are not aware of the potential contribution of America's Marine Highway system to decreasing congestion and emissions by moving freight from roadways to waterways. MARAD, through the Marine Highways Cooperative, is developing internet-based tools to help State and local transportation planners accurately determine the environmental benefits of diverting freight to Marine Highway services.[121]

The tools will calculate predicted reductions in specific harmful emissions, energy use, and congestion that can be achieved through greater use of this mode.

This information will enable State and local decision makers to recognize and promote water transportation projects within their jurisdictions.

Reducing Border Congestion – United States/Canada/Mexico Trilateral Working Group

In April 2006, the United States, Canada, and Mexico signed a Trilateral Agreement to cooperate in the development of Marine Highway systems in North America. As part of this agreement, the three participants formed a steering committee to "build an active relationship between the Participants" focused on enhanced use of water transportation. Although progress was initially slow, MARAD is using the agreement as a framework to reinvigorate the three-nation maritime partnership and identify and pursue opportunities aimed at reducing cross-border congestion. The steering committee will also attempt to mitigate any impediments to freight and passenger movements by water between the three countries. Staff-level meetings of the steering committee took place in January and June 2009. A meeting of the principals is scheduled for January 2011. The agenda for this meeting is to focus efforts to develop short sea services and remove impediments to such services so that they can relieve heavily congested border crossings between the United States and Canada and Mexico.

Outreach – America's Marine Highway Program Website

MARAD has completely reconfigured its America's Marine Highway Program website to provide visitors with the most up-to-date information about Marine Highway services, research on the topic, policy decisions, and other important information for shippers, operators, transportation officials, workers, and the public.[122] It contains up-to-date news and bulletins on the Program and new services, a complete inventory of existing Marine Highway services that shippers can utilize immediately, and arguably the most complete library of available studies, reports and plans related to the Marine Highway. This website, updated frequently, is an essential part of the agency's outreach effort to publicize and promote expanded use of water transportation.

OTHER PROGRESS – MARINE HIGHWAY SERVICES

As part of the development of the America's Marine Highway Program, MARAD has been providing direct support to Marine Highway services that serve as pilot projects on the east, Gulf, and west coasts of the United States.

54   U.S. Department of Transportation, Maritime Administration

These projects, the foremost of which are described below, provide tangible examples of the benefits that expansion of the America's Marine Highway system could offer; the viability of and challenges facing Marine Highway services in the commercial transportation market; and how the Federal government can play an important role in their development. The projects have also been the recipients of Marine Highway Project designations or "Grants for Transportation Investment Generating Economic Recovery" under the American Recovery and Reinvestment Act of 2009.

It should be noted that the services described below represent only a few examples of Marine Highway business models. There are, in fact, a variety of potentially successful business models for Marine Highway operators to use as they expand their presence in the nation's transportation system. These business models can range from high-volume line haul services to services aimed at niche or custom markets, such as the carriage of oversized, overweight, or hazardous cargoes (see text box below on Marine Highway Business Models).

East Coast Project – Norfolk to Richmond, VA

The "64 Express" is a container-on-barge service that began operation on December 1, 2008. This service, which was in planning for several years, operates weekly between Norfolk and Richmond, VA. In its first year, this water service was originally projected to shift more than 4,000 containers from trucks that would have used Hampton Boulevard in Norfolk and Interstate 64 (I-64), roads that are well-known for congestion and gridlock. In actuality, after a year in operation, the service had exceeded the projected volume by 50 percent, shifting over 6,000 containers to water service.

The project became a reality when MARAD hosted a meeting in 2007 between the prospective service provider and the Richmond Area MPO. The Richmond Area MPO, recognizing the potential benefits of this service, successfully incorporated the project within its regional long range transportation plan and convinced State and local decision makers of the advantages of utilizing Congestion Mitigation and Air Quality (CMAQ) program funding to help establish the service. The Richmond Area MPO obligated $2.25 million in CMAQ funds over three years to support this service through its initial start-up phase. Critically, the project has support from a team that includes, in addition to MARAD and the Richmond Area MPO, the Virginia Port Authority, the Port of Richmond, Norfolk Tug, the mayor of Norfolk, the Hampton Roads MPO, the Virginia DOT, and FHWA. The team's vision is to provide a sustainable service at the lowest cost possible to reduce congestion and energy use, improve air quality, and provide relief to highway maintenance costs – specifically those public benefits that are generally not reflected in private sector transportation decisions but which are worth capturing if their value exceeds the public costs of obtaining them.

The "64 Express" service is projected to shift 29,000 containers from congested roads by its third year and as many as 60,000 containers by the fifth year. The tugs used for this operation have modern, clean-burning, fuel efficient engines which use ultra-low sulfur diesel fuel. By the third year, in addition to reducing congestion, the service will reduce harmful emissions of nitrogen oxide, volatile organic compounds, and carbon monoxide by more than 70 tons a day and reduce highway wear and tear. At less than one-third the fuel consumption of trucks, each one-way trip made by the vessel consumes about 1,100 gallons of fuel, compared to about 3,300 gallons that trucks would have burned to carry the same volume of cargo.[123]

MARAD remains fully engaged in the project, coordinating and promoting the service among stakeholders. On September 20, 2010, the USDOT awarded a $1.1 million Marine Highway Grant to the project for the purchase of two barges. The service between Hampton Roads and Richmond will grow to three sailings each week and will start a new inter-terminal barge shuttle between terminals in Hampton Roads.

West Coast Project – Oakland to Stockton and West Sacramento, CA

This container-on-barge service will link the port of Oakland to the port of Stockton and the port of West Sacramento – a key gateway to California's Central Valley, one of the nation's largest agricultural export regions, and home to one of the nation's largest import distribution centers. Once operational, the service will help to relieve congestion along the I-880, I-580, I-205, and I5 highway corridors between the ports and produce other public benefits.

The initial concept for this service was developed as a result of a meeting between MARAD and a private investment group in early 2007. Seizing upon the interest expressed by the private investment group, and at their request, MARAD hosted a workshop at the port of Oakland to begin planning and bring the primary stakeholders together. Shippers, operators, port authorities, terminal operators, environmentalists, and representatives from the California Department of Transportation met to assess the advantages that a new Marine Highway service would offer. They considered cost savings to local shippers, benefits for importers and exporters (e.g., ability to move more goods in containers without exceeding road weight limits), and the public benefits the State of California is seeking. Among these public benefits are reduced miles of truck travel on congested regional highways; less wear-and-tear on highways and bridges by removing heavy and overweight loads; lower fuel consumption by shipping goods via barge rather than via exclusive truck movements; reduced GHG production and improved air quality by reducing diesel emissions from trucks; and improved public safety by reducing truck traffic.

In September 2009, the ports of Oakland, Stockton, and West Sacramento submitted an application to the Secretary for funding of this Marine Highway service under the terms of the Grants for Transportation Investment Generating Economic Recovery (TIGER) Discretionary Grants program.[124] Specifically, the ports sought TIGER funds for the installation of a combination of berth improvements, mobile harbor cranes, container loading facilities, container yard paving, rail track construction, and the procurement of a barge to support the service. These facilities will initially accommodate Marine Highway services traveling once weekly between the two inland ports to Oakland. On February 17, 2010, the Secretary awarded a TIGER Discretionary Grant of $30 million to the ports for this project, acknowledging the public benefits cited above.[125] Initial construction began in late October 2010.[126]

Gulf Coast Project – Brownsville, TX to Manatee, FL

In mid-December 2008 SeaBridge Freight, a new container-on-barge service, began to shift containers from trucks that would otherwise have traveled on highways I-10 and I-75 along the Gulf Coast. This Marine Highway service began with the capacity to remove about 600 truck trips each week from this major east-west highway corridor, which passes through several urban areas, including Houston, TX, New Orleans, LA, and Mobile, AL. At over 1,300 highway miles per truck trip avoided, this equates to approximately 800,000 large truck highway miles saved every week. The first round-trip voyage transported 1,800 tons of freight, including several oversized and overweight loads of the types that are responsible for much of the highway and bridge wear and tear when transported by trucks. The service also transported several tank trucks containing hazardous materials, demonstrating the Marine Highway's potential to divert the most dangerous cargo around major urban areas.

MARAD assisted the operator in evaluating technologically advanced clean-burning ultra low sulfur fuel and bio-diesel as an alternative energy source in the near future. One source reports the following overall benefits of the SeaBridge Freight service:[127]

- Savings of more than 70,000 gallons of diesel fuel per voyage or more than four million gallons of diesel fuel per year;
- Total cost per pound of freight that is 29 percent less than the trucking alternative; and
- A reduction of over 50 percent of fuel on a per ton-mile basis compared to rail.

SeaBridge Freight was the first Marine Highway service provider to earn the EPA's SmartWay Transport Partnership status.[128]

Unfortunately, as is often the case with new business ventures, the company ceased operations in November 2010 and closed its offices in January 2011 because it could not raise the funding necessary to execute its long-term business strategy.

The company's experience demonstrated, however, that there is a market for an all-water freight service between the Port of Brownsville and Port Manatee. MARAD is working closely with these ports to reestablish this service under a new operator, and the ports have reported that there are several potential providers interested in restarting the service.

Marine Highway Business Models

There are many business models that can be used to enter or expand water transportation services offered on America's Marine Highway. Each business model has implications for the scale and cost of operations, the type of services, and the equipment and personnel that the Marine Highway operator will offer to customers.

Some of the models described below are not mutually exclusive, but most Marine Highway operators will likely specialize in one of the following model types:

- Line-haul water transportation service wholesalers – A principal benefit of water transportation is its ability to offer low-cost transportation and avoid congested roads and rail. To realize the full cost savings of water, it is helpful to operate fully-loaded, larger vessels.

  One method of acquiring sufficient cargo for this purpose is to wholesale the water transportation service to truck, rail, and intermodal companies who can use their established marketing systems to fill larger vessels with appropriate cargo. In this model, the Marine Highway serves as an "additional lane on the highway". Such services could include RoRo operations along the I-95 corridor or from the Gulf Coast to the Mid-Atlantic States.

- Transshipment services for international exporters and importers – Marine Highway operators can transship international containers to and from congested ports to smaller, less congested ports that have good highway and rail access and adequate container storage space. This service, which can serve relatively short haul markets, could alleviate congestion in large port cities and in the ports themselves. The demand for this service will likely grow (particularly after the Panama Canal expansion is complete in 2014) as the largest post-Panamax containerships reduce their port calls only to a few first tier ports, from which container cargo could be transferred to second tier ports by water.

- Full service water transportation retailers – U.S. water transportation companies already offer sophisticated door-to-door intermodal services, particularly for services to Alaska, Hawaii, Puerto Rico, and along coastal routes.

  Because Marine Highway services must compete with landside intermodal providers in many cases, acquiring sufficient volumes of cargo to fill ships offering regular scheduled service along coast routes can be difficult.

- Hub-and-spoke services – Service providers would operate trunk-feeder services over hub-and-spoke networks, enabling consolidation of sufficient cargo volumes at hub locations to reach destinations that would be uneconomic to serve with line haul services.

  The success of this business model would be contingent on significantly reducing cargo transfer costs at hub port facilities.

America's Marine Highway: Report to Congress

- Niche market services – Customers often need to move oversized or overweight cargo. Although there are means to move such cargo by land, particularly by rail, water transportation is well suited to deliver even the largest such cargoes with few adverse impacts to infrastructure or requirements for special permits. This business model is especially viable in regions for which multiple State permits to move the freight on highways would otherwise be needed (e.g., New England), or in areas with aging infrastructure that may have weight restrictions.

- Hazmat services – The movement of hazardous materials can pose particular challenges to shippers (see report section on Public Safety and Security). Truck movements of hazmat must typically be made by specially-trained drivers, making long-haul truck movements expensive. Marine Highway operators can provide specially-trained vessel crews and drayage operators, as well as on-board cargo monitoring systems, to move cargo at lower unit cost, while avoiding high population areas and conflicting road traffic.

- Factory-to-factory services – Marine Highway operations can target the movement of dedicated products from producer to distributor or from factory to factory. These shipments are most tenable if water can provide direct point-to-point routing and bypass bottlenecks in highways and rail. In such instances, the Marine Highway can be effective even over relatively short hauls along waterways and coastal areas.

Even within the business models described above, there are different strategies for meeting customer demand. For instance, an operator may choose to go after higher value, time-sensitive cargo that would require a door-to-door transit comparable to land-based modes through the use of RoRo vessels operating on daily frequencies, or deploy conventional containerships on less frequent schedules to carry heavy or lower value cargoes at lower costs. Regardless of the business model used, Marine Highway operators would likely need to provide services such as chassis management, tracking and security, container and trailer storage, and other value-added features to attract wholesale and retail customers.

Source: Based on information in Global Insight, Four Corridor Case Studies of Short-Sea Shipping Services: Short-Sea Shipping Business Case Analysis, prepared for the U.S. Department of Transportation, Office of the Secretary/Maritime Administration, Ref. DTOS59-04-Q-00069, August 15, 2006.

IMPEDIMENTS TO NEW AND EXPANDED MARINE HIGHWAY SERVICES

America's Marine Highway offers the promise of providing much-needed freight and passenger transportation capacity in a manner that would reduce surface traffic congestion and support other critical national objectives with regard to safety, security, energy, and the environment. At the same time, the current use of water transportation, particularly for container and trailer freight shipments, falls well behind highway and rail movements.

Largely, Marine Highway services are comprised of the following chief elements: infrastructure, vessels, and equipment; operations and administration; and a market for cargoes. This section will summarize by category some of the factors affecting these elements that have worked to limit the greater commercial use of water transportation. It will also highlight issues pertaining to the lack of public awareness on the contribution that Marine Highway services can make to our transportation system and quality of life.[129]

Infrastructure, Vessel, and Equipment Needs

While Marine Highway services are relatively easy to initiate at the majority of the nation's port facilities, highly efficient services require specialized equipment in many instances. For example, at smaller ports, specialized gantry cranes may need to be installed to efficiently load and unload marine container barges. Many moderate-sized port facilities possess adequate space to accommodate start-up Marine Highway services but may have to make certain modifications (such as wharf rehabilitation, berth improvements, paving, fencing, and staging area development) and acquire additional shoreside equipment (such as specialized cranes, forklifts, hostlers, tractors, and top pick forklifts) for these operations. The European experience shows that the major investment costs, particularly at inland barge container terminals, consist of infrastructure (wharf construction and grounds) and equipment (cranes and internal transport vehicles).[130]

The initial acquisition cost of port facility and cargo handling equipment can be a significant barrier to market entry for Marine Highway services. Initially, such services often involve relatively small volumes of cargo that must bear the full costs of paying for the new port infrastructure. This high fixed cost, which must be passed on to shippers, places Marine Highway services at a competitive disadvantage relative to established land-based modes. Particularly for startup Marine Highway operations, Federal, State and local financial support, through grants or loans, may be necessary to make the investments possible (see section below on Potential Legislative Actions to Support America's Marine Highway). In Europe, many terminals have been set up with government subsidies, which lower the initial investment costs.[131]

Special adaptations may be needed at the nation's largest ports. Existing docks at ports that handle large international containerships may not be compatible with RoRo vessels. The largest, most congested ports may not have available dock and yard space for loading and unloading smaller vessels. Moreover, Marine Highway vessels may have to call at multiple terminals at the same port, requiring more time in port to load and unload containers and trailers.

Developing and expanding infrastructure at ports and terminals can have substantial environmental impacts, including to water/marine resources and habitats. These activities, which include construction, operations, and maintenance activities (e.g., dredging), need to be conducted in conformance with environmentally-protective regulatory and programmatic frameworks to address environmental protection and sustainability.

Current vessels serving the U.S. domestic trades reflect a variety of types, ages, configurations, speeds, and cargo handling capabilities. Some older vessels have less efficient engines, burn bunker fuel that is less clean than diesel fuels, and generally are more expensive to operate. The variability of ship characteristics within the U.S. fleet also creates inefficiency when transporting and transferring cargoes within an intermodal system. Standardization of vessel designs or design requirements would facilitate the ability of service providers, ports, and shippers to plan, implement, or utilize America's Marine Highway on a national scale. Standardization of vessel designs or design requirements would also facilitate series construction of vessels, which would lower vessel construction costs. Ideally, standardized vessels intended to transport containers and trailers as an alternative to land-based carriers should be designed to minimize vessel operating costs and maximize the speed and efficiency of cargo loading, storage, and unloading operations. They must also be designed and operated in a manner that supports Federal, State, and local environmental objectives.

Standardization of Marine Highway vessel and equipment design is especially important because it would allow ports to build and modify facilities to efficiently meet the specific needs of the vessels. In fact, so important is the relationship between vessel and port terminal design that

62   U.S. Department of Transportation, Maritime Administration

MARAD has proposed research projects to develop standardized designs for Marine Highway vessels and terminal facilities that would be conducted in coordination with each other (see section above on Marine Highway Research). Only through coordinated, standardized design guidelines for vessels and port terminal facilities can the full cost-effectiveness of the Marine Highway system be realized. For instance, the development of a standardized RoRo vessel design would be coordinated with a standardized port terminal design that would enable the ramp(s) of the vessel to be deployed efficiently while in port.

MARAD anticipates that its participation in promoting standardization will yield significant transportation, safety, and environmental benefits to the public at modest overall cost to the government. As noted earlier, new vessel demand supported through design standardization would also provide the shipbuilding community with the opportunity to construct more vessels, helping to sustain the nation' shipbuilding industrial base (see earlier section on Maintaining National Shipbuilding Capabilities).

Finally, the development of standardized vessel and terminal designs or design requirements would explore the incorporation of National Defense Features, particularly for RoRo-type vessels and the port facilities that serve them. The inclusion of such features (e.g., reinforced decks, cranes, and ramps) could justify sharing of some costs by the Federal government, such as through the National Defense Sealift Fund for vessels.[132] More broadly, some continuing level of government intervention may be needed to design new vessels and terminal infrastructure that are also suitable for national defense purposes, as well as to initiate and sustain orders for the same.

Operations and Administration

Basic categories of Marine Highway operating costs include fuel, maintenance, labor, insurance, stores, stevedoring[133], administration, port fees, drayage[134], and other expenses (such as pilotage[135] requirements at deepwater ports). Keeping these costs as low as possible is important to the success of Marine Highway services. A study done in 2006 of potential Marine Highway markets concluded that, in several important markets, short sea operators must obtain optimal ("best in class") performance from management, crew, and equipment if they are to be price and service competitive with land-based modes.[136] The study assumed the use of efficient, relatively low cost vessels and engines, reduced crew sizes, modern navigation and communications equipment, significant cargo volumes, and efficient cargo transfer and stowage systems to obtain "best in class" performance. The study did not quantify the value of external costs and benefits to the public associated with shipper decisions to use each respective transportation mode.

An especially critical component of Marine Highway operating costs is loading and unloading the vessels at ports. There are two primary methods for such services as they apply to non-bulk freight: lift-on/lift-off (LoLo) techniques using cranes and roll-on/roll-off (RoRo) techniques for cargoes being transported by truck aboard chasses.

In LoLo operations, a container must be moved on and off of a vessel at least two times in a shipment – once at the port of departure and again at the port of arrival. The cost of handling containers is highly dependent on the use of optimal crane and equipment types for expected container volumes, the number of containers transshipped at the port, and equipment costs. In many ports, efforts to reduce air pollution attributable to cargo handling operations will also affect the types and costs of cranes and other equipment. Europe has explored advanced concepts to mitigate port handling costs, including: automated cranes; unmanned, self-service terminals at inland ports; specialized self-loading and unloading container vessels; and other innovative approaches to lowering costs and expediting loading and unloading of containers.[137] Higher container volumes allow for more efficient crane equipment and operations and therefore lower the unit costs of handling containers. Similarly, investment in specialized handling equipment can greatly lower handling costs, making it possible to size a crane for an expected future volume of containers without overburdening the initial volumes with excessively high capital costs. In general, container barge vessels and self-propelled containerships, which generally cost less than RoRos and stow cargo more efficiently, will have operational advantages over RoRos in high volume markets, particularly if optimal equipment is deployed and handling costs are reduced from current levels.

RoRo loading and unloading costs can cost less than a container transfer at smaller ports that do not have the freight volumes needed to justify efficient container handling systems.[138] In such ports, the cost savings from reduced port cargo-handling costs and faster vessel and trailer turn-times may more than offset the more effective vessel capacity utilization provided by containerships versus RoRo vessels.[139]

Currently, with existing port infrastructure, the combined cargo transfer cost for a single Marine Highway shipment can exceed $250 per container or trailer, even before marine transportation and drayage costs. When compared to competing truck shipment costs of approximately $1,000 per trailer for door-to-door service along a coast route, these transfer costs and associated time delays stand out as impediments to robust growth of demand for Marine Highway services. As discussed above, the use of standardized and coordinated vessel and port terminal designs could mitigate Marine Highway operating costs. Similarly, appropriate vessel types, correctly-sized equipment, and targeted assistance could also facilitate the growth of Marine Highway services. All of these potential methods to mitigate cargo handling costs offer promise for expanding the use of America's Marine Highway.

Impact of the Jones Act on Marine Highway Costs

Cabotage is the transport of cargo or passengers between two points in the same country by a vessel or an aircraft registered in another country. Permission to engage in cabotage is, in general, restricted in every country. In the United States, cabotage restrictions apply to domestic water, land, and air transportation.

The Jones Act, which is the popular name for section 27 of the Merchant Marine Act of 1920 (46 U.S.C. 883), requires that all waterborne shipping between points within the United States be carried by vessels built in the United States, owned by U.S. citizens (at least 75 percent), and manned with U.S. citizen crews. Under the Jones Act, all domestic water transportation providers compete under uniform laws and regulations that protect their crews and cargo and the natural environment, creating an even playing field. Of the 39,866 vessels (including 32,184 barges and 5,707 tugs) in the U.S.-flag privately owned fleet as of 2008, all but 93 vessels were Jones Act qualified vessels.[140] The great majority of active U.S. mariners are employed in Jones Act trades.

Some have suggested that the costs associated with domestic-build requirements for Jones Act impede the ability of Marine Highway services to compete with land-based transportation modes, which are able to purchase vehicles from foreign builders. This impediment is claimed because some vessel types can cost significantly more to purchase from U.S. shipyards than if purchased from abroad, particularly vessels that are not produced in large numbers by U.S. shipyards. While vessel capital costs are clearly a factor in establishing Marine Highway operations, each transportation mode has its own sets of regulations, tolls, fees, common carrier obligations, etc., that impact its ability to economically compete with other modes, and cross-modal comparisons should consider the full range and impact of these factors.

With regard to the effect of the Jones Act domestic-build requirement on the competitiveness of Marine Highway services, GAO found mixed impacts. Short sea operators in the U.S. northeast reported to GAO that the domestic-build requirement was not a significant concern because they use tug-and-barge vessels in which the U.S. and foreign-built versions are more similarly priced than U.S. and foreign-built self-propelled vessels.[141] On the other hand, GAO reports that Gulf Coast operators said that the high capital costs of purchasing new U.S.-flag vessels affected their ability to expand operations and keep shipping prices competitive with trucking.[142] Generally, Jones Act-related costs for vessel acquisition will be largest for operators requiring self-propelled coastal vessels which the U.S. shipyards manufacture in small volumes. Such shipyards cannot take advantage of the efficiencies of scale production afforded by large series and common design orders, and thus are often challenged in maintaining a trained, experienced workforce. Industry sources also disagree on the potential for reduced costs using foreign-built vessels in such operations.[143]

Lack of Cargo – Market Perceptions

There has been a general reluctance of shippers and freight forwarders to make use of water transportation for domestic container and trailer freight movements. Traditional perceptions of slow domestic maritime services that do not operate on fixed schedules have contributed to this reluctance. Current and future Marine Highway operators must demonstrate that they can provide frequent and reliable service to a wide range of destinations. Demonstrating high quality service is an important goal of the pilot projects that MARAD has been supporting as well as other recently-designated Marine Highway Projects (see sections on Other Progress – Marine Highway Services and Initial Progress: Description of Activities Conducted under the America's Marine Highway Program, above).

An emphasis on schedule and service reliability of Marine Highway service is of particular importance. One survey of shippers conducted for the Coalition of Alabama Waterway Associations found that 48 percent of the respondents assigned the greatest importance to reliability, 38 percent reported cost as their highest priority, and 15 percent reported transit time as their highest priority.[144] Although transit time is often stressed as an advantage of land-based modes, reliability is often more important, particularly in "just-in-time" inventory systems. Shipments that arrive too early incur handling and storage costs, just as late shipments cost shippers through the inability to get products to market as intended. Moreover, supply chain managers using modern cargo tracking technologies can make effective use of the Marine Highway to accommodate "inventory in transit," taking advantage of the fact that carrying inventory in transit often costs less than carrying the same inventory in a warehouse.[145] In the increasingly sophisticated supply chain system, Marine Highway offers strong potential to improve, at comparatively low cost, the overall efficiency of domestic freight transportation through regularly scheduled vessel calls and efficient port operations.

Recent studies have identified a broad range of strategies to maximize the reliability of Marine Highway operations. Such strategies include the development of sound business plans that clearly identify market characteristics and customer needs and ensure appropriate capitalization and financing. Reliability is also enhanced by operating vessels with appropriate capacities and characteristics to serve identified markets, establishing clear ownership and control of vessels and other assets, avoiding overly complex service routes, employing experienced crews, arranging efficient terminal and stevedoring services, and other factors.[146] Advanced technologies are now available to allow Marine Highway operators to navigate waterways more efficiently and deliver cargo faster and more reliably even under difficult weather conditions.[147]

Other actions that could make the Marine Highway more attractive to shippers would be for the private sector to offer "value added" services at port terminals, including coordinating and synchronizing flows of containers to different regions, freight warehousing and assembling, organization of drayage operations, and other logistical and shipper support services.[148] These services would facilitate what can otherwise be a complex administration process of arranging connections and increase the reliability and utility of Marine Highway service to customers.[149]

Shippers must also have confidence that the interface between water and land-based shipping will be relatively seamless. Investing in port and last-mile-to-port infrastructure to eliminate delays associated with intermodal transfers will be vital to the future of America's Marine Highway. The seamless integration of waterborne transportation into the landside networks of highway and rail will also serve to optimize Federal surface transportation investments and provide for greater short-haul trucking opportunities.

The Importance of Public Benefits

As noted in the introduction to this report, the decision by a shipper to use a transportation mode is generally influenced chiefly, if not solely, by the monetary costs and benefits that the shipper expects to accrue as a result of that decision. When considering water transportation, the shipper will assess the reliability of the service, the freight bill, the schedule frequency, the freight transit time, and other factors that ultimately affect the profitability of the company. The shipper generally will be much less influenced by costs and benefits of his or her transportation decision that do not affect profitability (so called "external" costs and benefits).

Thus, when considering a Marine Highway service, the shipper will consider the value of any reduced delay or improved delivery reliability to his or her cargo from avoiding a congested roadway, but will not consider the value of the potential delay savings and travel time reliability improvements to members of the public who continue to use the roadway after the removal of the shipper's cargo from the traffic stream. Nor would the shipper normally be influenced by reduced emissions, lower national energy usage, improved public safety, or other benefits to the public associated with his or her choice to use Marine Highway services unless he or she is actually compensated for them (such as through reduced insurance costs). EPA's SmartWay Transport Partnership Program does, however, help shippers and carriers to see opportunities for lower costs through reduced fuel consumption and the benefits of social recognition for environmental responsibility that they might otherwise not have considered.

When considering public investments in Marine Highway infrastructure, the public should be aware of the costs it may incur if investments in this infrastructure are not made. A direct dialog with the public on this issue is warranted. For instance, the European Commission, which has an active policy to promote and assist short sea shipping with public resources, finds that:

> This form of transport mode is highly efficient in terms of environmental performance and energy efficiency. It has the potential to solve road congestion problems affecting many parts of the European continent. All the studies point out the necessity of encouraging short sea shipping to meet the goal of the European sustainable transport policy.[150]

If the U.S. public realizes the social value of water transportation, it would likely be willing to assist in the development of vessel or port infrastructure or

68   U.S. Department of Transportation, Maritime Administration

other aspects of water transportation so as to lower relative costs to shippers and encourage to greater use of this mode. It may also be willing to use its influence as a consumer group to drive more environmentally sustainable shipping practices, if options like the Marine Highway were more well-known. Accordingly, shipper companies seeking to market themselves as environmentally-responsible actors whose operations (as well as the products themselves) are considered "green" may look to Marine Highway services as a means of attracting customers or consumers who share these values or desire to obtain the same public environmental benefits.

Buy-In from Public and Transportation Planners

Generally, researchers have found that regional transportation planners direct their attention to regional highway and transit investments and are less focused on interstate freight issues. This focus is due to many factors, including perceptions that many of the benefits of freight investments fall outside of the planning organization's jurisdiction as compared to other transportation investments such as new roads, intersections, etc. that benefit local commuters; the benefits accrue to the private sector and therefore should be funded by the private sector; planning and funding are difficult to coordinate among multiple State and local authorities; and Federal funding, which is often tied to a single mode, can be difficult to apply to multimodal freight projects.[151] The lack of a national freight policy further complicates efforts by State and local planners to support the national freight system. When transportation planners do address interstate or regional freight issues, not all planners are aware of the capacity and environmental contributions that the Marine Highway can offer.[152]

In response, MARAD is striving to raise the profile of America's Marine Highway among planners and assist them in understanding, funding, and supporting Marine Highway freight projects. Both from its headquarters and through its ten Gateway Offices, located in major port cities across the nation, MARAD will continue to work with State Departments of Transportation and MPOs to incorporate Marine Highway services (including ferries) in State, multi-State, and regional transportation plans. It will also encourage them to consider land uses (such as waterfront industrial parks or the preservation of working waterfronts) that would facilitate the success of Marine Highway services. MARAD provides these authorities with information on potential funding sources for Marine Highway projects, such as the Congestion

Mitigation and Air Quality program for projects that reduce emissions and are based in designated air quality nonattainment or maintenance areas, the Ferry Boat Discretionary Program for passenger ferry services, Marine Highway Grants, and TIGER grants. Similarly, MARAD works with other USDOT modal administrations to facilitate and support port and passenger ferry projects. As part of USDOT, MARAD communicates with other Federal departments and agencies to promote awareness of Marine Highway transportation needs and options and seek out collaborative opportunities.

The ability of MARAD to promote Marine Highway services is limited, however, by its available resources and diverse responsibilities. The water transportation industry must greatly improve efforts to educate the public, shippers, legislators, and transportation planners about the public and private benefits of the Marine Highway for the movement of goods and passengers. Although such efforts often take place at a company-to-company level, it is nonetheless beneficial when educational efforts are coordinated at an industry coalition level. Well-known coalitions exist to support individual transportation modes and services, including highways, trucking, transit, and rail, but there is currently no dominant coalition entity that advocates the Marine Highway on behalf of water transportation industry as a whole.[153] A well-funded coalition with a concise message and a targeted, comprehensive marketing campaign could increase the visibility of the Marine Highway and secure more support for its expansion.

POTENTIAL LEGISLATIVE ACTIONS TO SUPPORT AMERICA'S MARINE HIGHWAY

Pursuant to Energy Act requirements, the Secretary has consulted with members of the transportation community to develop proposals for short-term incentives to encourage the use of America's Marine Highway. This section summarizes the principal short-term incentives that key stakeholders in the transportation community identified, as compiled by MARAD, and provides explanations of how and why such incentives could accelerate the expansion of America's Marine Highway. These incentives do not address broader policies that might incentivize Marine Highway services such as a cap-and-trade regime for CO2 and criteria pollutants or greater use of pricing and congestion fees for land-based transportation, both of which would have ramifications far beyond the greater use of water transportation. Combinations of short-term incentives targeted at Marine Highway service providers along with broader policies to reduce emissions and fuel consumption at a national level would likely have a greater effect in encouraging Marine Highway services than short-term incentives alone.

It should be emphasized that the incentives listed below are suggestions from the transportation community and are not necessarily endorsed by MARAD, USDOT, or the Administration. Furthermore, these incentives would require implementation through legislation (where authority is needed) and regulation. Useful suggestions for administrative actions that MARAD received during its consultations with the stakeholders either have been or are being implemented, as described in an earlier section of this report (see Initial Progress: Description of Activities Conducted under the America's Marine Highway Program).

Where incentives involve new funding or offsets to Federal tax revenue, this discussion does not attempt to identify potential revenue sources. However, as a general principle, the Administration has proposed that any federally-funded transportation investments be designed primarily to achieve the realization of public benefits not otherwise obtainable through purely market transactions. The America's Marine Highway initiative has great potential to provide many public benefits as described in greater detail earlier in this report. In addition, any federally-funded market incentives should be designed to encourage innovative financing methods and support the Program's objective that Marine Highway services be viable as longterm ventures to provide reliability of service as a mode of transportation.

As the notion of expanded Marine Highway services is not a new one, stakeholders provided many suggestions. Foremost, many of the primary suggestions involved using Federal tax policy to influence cargo demand on the America's Marine Highway. Such broad policy shifts could help our nation realize many of the public benefits associated with Marine Highway services that are not currently being captured. Further, they can do so in a way that minimizes the risk of conveying an unfair advantage to one Marine Highway carrier relative to another.

The options suggested by the transportation community for short-term (up to three years) incentives and legislative actions focus on three key stakeholder groups in the Marine Transportation System:

- *Cargo owners and surface transportation service providers:*[154] Many in the maritime industry have expressed that increasing the demand for waterborne transportation should be the first priority of incentives. New demand creates a strong incentive for the provision of vessel and port capacity and will ultimately benefit all key stakeholder groups through direct cost savings, higher frequencies, better service, and more revenue.

- *Vessel owners and operators:* Vessel owners and operators face obstacles in startup risk, the cost of vessel construction, and shipper reluctance to change established routes and methods. Knowing that our nation is willing to invest to achieve public benefits associated with Marine Highway services will help encourage similar private sector investments in long-life cycle assets like new vessels. Several incentives below are aimed at these factors.

- *Shoreside Infrastructure Owners and Operators:* Marine Highway services require adequate shoreside infrastructure that may represent a change to established port operations. Many of the major ports are configured to handle international shipping containers but not RoRo trailers, and smaller ports often lack the equipment to handle containerized cargo. Moreover, little coordination exists to ensure standardization of infrastructure and equipment among these ports.

Harbor Maintenance Tax

The Harbor Maintenance Tax (HMT) is an *ad valorem* tax of 0.125 percent of cargo value (i.e., $1.25 per $1,000 in cargo value) assessed to the shippers receiving inbound (imports or domestic) cargo at a U.S. port. It can add an average of $60 per forty-foot container to shipping costs.[155] The tax is deposited into the Harbor Maintenance Trust Fund, which is now used to fund harbor maintenance activities, primarily maintenance dredging.

Stakeholders have requested that the HMT be waived for non-bulk cargo shipments between U.S. domestic mainland ports or from Canadian ports on the Great Lakes or St. Lawrence Seaway to U.S. ports. They believe that the tax may, in these situations, serve as a disincentive to transport by water where the cost of land transportation is comparable. Legislation was introduced in the 111th Congress to provide such waivers.156

Customs Processing of Inbound Containers on Great Lakes

The geographical boundaries of America's Marine Highway, as defined in the Energy Act, includes the shipment of containers and trailers loaded at a port in the United States and unloaded either at another port in the United States or at a port in Canada located in the Great Lakes Saint Lawrence Seaway System; or loaded at a port in Canada located in the Great Lakes Saint Lawrence Seaway System and unloaded at a port in the United States." There is a significant barrier, however, to the ability of Marine Highway services to carry containerized cargo from Canada to the United States. By regulation, manifests of containerized cargo inbound from Canadian and other foreign ports must be sent electronically to U.S. Customs and Border Protection (CBP) 24 hours before *loading* of the cargo onto the vessel.[157] Foreign air, rail, and truck manifests, on the other hand, need be sent to CBP only 4 hours, 2 hours, and 1 hour, respectively, before arrival in the United States.[158] This different notification requirement can cause delays of many hours for container shipments from Canada on the Marine Highway that other transportation modes do not experience. Treating waterborne container shipments from Canada in a manner comparable to land-based shipments of the same containers for purposes of application of this rule would remove a major obstacle to increasing Marine Highway services on the Great Lakes.

Shipper Tax Credits

Companies in the business of shipping freight, including brokers, freight forwarders, rail carriers, trucking companies, and third-party logistics providers, may be reluctant to re-direct their routing to a new service even if they stand to gain potential benefits or cost savings as it introduces new delivery risks with which they are less familiar. A shipper often operates under negotiated contracts with trucking and railroad companies for many years and may not be willing to jeopardize effective working relationships to move to a new Marine Highway service, particularly if the service provider does not have an established performance record.[159] Some have suggested the creation of Federal incentives to shippers to consider and use water transportation through mileage-based rebates or corporate tax credits for each container or trailer that moves by water. The rebates could be linked to the value of public benefits associated with the decision to select water transportation. Such a program could be applied nationally, subject to a letter of eligibility from MARAD, or could be made specific to designated Marine Highway Corridors or Projects that alleviate severe highway congestion.

Focusing eligibility on specific corridors or projects could help to ensure that such credits would provide the greatest public benefit. It also offers a controlled environment and limited scope to evaluate the true costs and benefits of the incentive along with any intended and unintended implications that may emerge. The primary beneficiaries of a rebate program would be cargo owners and surface transportation service providers, but the resulting increase in usage of water transportation would also benefit vessel and shoreside infrastructure owners and operators.

Investment Tax Credits

Investment tax credits are reductions in the tax that companies pay on their profits if they invest in certain types of equipment or infrastructure. Private companies could receive a tax credit for qualified capital investments to start or expand a designated Marine Highway Project. Qualified expenditures could include design, construction, or modification of vessels, development or improvement of shoreside infrastructure, procurement of cargo handling equipment, intermodal connector development, or any investment that reduces fuel consumption or emissions for qualified expenditures.[160] Direct beneficiaries of investment tax credits would be vessel owners and operators and shoreside infrastructure owners.

Accelerated Depreciation

Some stakeholders have suggested that making investments in Marine Highway projects eligible for accelerated depreciation under Federal tax law would be a significant incentive to help expand America's Marine Highway. Accelerated depreciation allows a more rapid expensing of asset costs for tax purposes than is generally permitted. It offers the advantage of deferring the

74   U.S. Department of Transportation, Maritime Administration

payment of taxes which both reduces their present value to the investor and helps to maximize net income in the years immediately following asset purchases. The depreciation benefit is offset later in the form of reduced deductions, but when the operator is usually in a stronger position to accommodate the taxes. Such accelerated depreciation would have a maximum benefit in the first three years of operation, when a Marine Highway service is most likely to need cash flow in order to mature.

Matching Capital Grants

Stakeholders recommended the establishment of an America's Marine Highway matching capital grants program to fund projects that improve the efficiency and productivity of water transportation of passengers and freight (containers and trailers). Since MARAD initially queried stakeholders, several significant legislative actions have created a basis for such grants. These are as follows:

- Congress has specifically authorized "America's Short Sea Transportation Grants for the Development of Marine Highways" (implemented by MARAD in August 2010 as the Marine Highway Grants program).[161]
- Congress has appropriated up to $7 million in funding for the Marine Highway Grants program for FY 2010.[162]
- Congress authorized MARAD to establish a new Port Infrastructure Development Program.[163] The new program provides a framework for MARAD to receive and manage port improvement funds, coordinate with other Federal, State, and local agencies to expedite the environmental review processes for port projects, and provide technical assistance to port authorities or commissions.[164] To augment the ability of MARAD to work directly with ports, the program is established with a Port Infrastructure Development Fund to receive transfers of Federal, non-Federal, and private funds from entities that have specific agreements or contracts with MARAD. Grants of capital funds made by other USDOT agencies to eligible port projects under title 23 or chapter 53 of title 49 of the United States Code may now be transferred to this fund, subject to the written agreement of these agencies and the terms and eligibilities originally approved by those agencies.

- Congress provided up to $1.5 billion in the American Recovery and Reinvestment Act of 2009 (Recovery Act) to be used by USDOT to make discretionary grants for surface transportation investments (referred to as TIGER Discretionary Grants). Seven port-related projects benefiting Marine Highway services were among the 51 successful applicants for these grants in 2009-2010.[165] A similar discretionary grants program (referred to as TIGER II) was funded at $600 million in the Consolidated Appropriations Act of 2010.[166] Seven port-related projects were among the 42 successful applicants for TIGER II capital construction grant funds.

MARAD has gained valuable experience in administering grant programs. The agency provided extensive assistance to the Secretary in the recent evaluations of the TIGER Discretionary Grants and manages the 14 capital grants awarded to ports under the TIGER and TIGER II programs. MARAD also continues to administer the award of numerous matching capital grants to small shipyards under its Small Shipyard Assistance Grant Program. As such, it is well-prepared to administer matching capital grants under the above authorities or any similar future programs (such as a multimodal infrastructure bank), including for projects to improve the physical infrastructure of ports, terminals, and intermodal connectors. Matching capital grants under the new Marine Highway Grants initiative could extend to the purchase or lease of terminal equipment and construction or modification of vessels to increase energy efficiency and meet high environmental standards. Direct beneficiaries of matching capital grants would be vessel owners and operators and shoreside infrastructure owners.

MARAD's administration of existing grant programs also provides it with clear insight into the outcomes of the grant-funded projects. MARAD will monitor project outcomes to see if the projects accomplish their objectives of promoting use of Marine Highway services. Information of this type is vital to understanding the potential for success of larger future Federal investments in America's Marine Highway, including potential investments in new vessel designs or improved port facilities.

Marine Highway Title XI Loan Guarantees

The Title XI Federal Ship Financing Program, administered by MARAD, enables owners of eligible vessels and shipyards to obtain long-term capital financing with attractive terms by providing a full faith and credit guarantee of eligible debt obligations. When credit markets are constrained, this program has been particularly helpful to obtain long-term financing for vessels. Stakeholders have suggested modifications to the Title XI program to help introduce more environmentally sustainable vessels into the U.S. fleet and stimulate growth in U.S. shipyard jobs. Potential changes to the program could prioritize Marine Highway vessels, allow Title XI to be used for directly-related shoreside facility improvements, revise debt/equity and working capital requirements (responding to the needs of startup operators), and include a mandate to conform to high environmental standards. Any such changes, however, would need to be made in a manner that would not jeopardize the financial integrity of the Title IX program. Direct beneficiaries of Title XI loan guarantees would be vessel owners and operators and, potentially, shoreside infrastructure owners.

Marine Transportation Infrastructure Finance and Innovation Act

The Transportation Infrastructure Finance and Innovation Act (TIFIA) is a Federal program that provides credit assistance for significant land transportation projects. Projects located within the boundary of a port terminal are eligible to receive TIFIA assistance provided that the project is limited to surface transportation infrastructure modifications that are necessary to facilitate direct intermodal interchange, transfer, and access into and out of the port. Additionally, projects must have eligible costs reasonably anticipated to total at least $50 million to be considered for TIFIA credit instruments, or alternatively, eligible project costs must equal 33⅓ percent or more of the State's Federal-aid highway apportionments for the most recently completed fiscal year, whichever is less. Other TIFIA eligibility thresholds apply, some of which would be difficult for many port projects to meet.[167] Some stakeholders have suggested that the creation of a smaller-scale maritime infrastructure-oriented program similar to TIFIA could help to fund port and terminal intermodal infrastructure, especially in small and medium-sized ports. These ports usually do not have projects which meet the minimum TIFIA eligibility requirements, such as projects of at least $50 million in scope. In addition, extending eligibility to cargo-handling equipment and other investments would be needed to accommodate Marine Highway projects.

CONCLUSION

As this report illustrates, the opportunity to more effectively balance our national transportation system – with numerous transportation services, including rail, road, and water – is attractive for a number of reasons. A balanced system that takes advantage of the relative strengths of each mode can better address the transportation challenges of growing surface congestion, aging infrastructure, and system repair and expansion. These challenges, combined with growing public pressure to improve the environment and the need to reduce our nation's dependence on petroleum fuels, make America's Marine Highway an attractive transportation choice. Furthermore, it can help our government's response to and recovery from emergencies and provide mobility resources to support national defense.

The expanded use of our waterways can only incrementally improve each of the challenges identified in this report. Moreover, there are many markets where highway and rail will remain the preferred or only choices. America's Marine Highway should, however, be viewed as a logical next step as we address our larger surface transportation and funding challenges. In many cases, these benefits can be quickly realized due to pre-existing port and waterway infrastructure and the rapid start-up times of Marine Highway services, particularly when compared to the time required to fund, engineer, construct, and repair much of our land-based transportation infrastructure system.

Despite significant progress in short sea container transportation in Europe and recent successful service startups here in the United States, America's Marine Highway must still overcome barriers before it can reach its potential. Disincentives to increased use of the Marine Highway include the unfamiliarity of shippers with this domestic transportation alternative, the lack of an established network of frequent service for container and trailer cargoes, the need for coordinated investment in port infrastructure and vessels, tax issues, and the fact that public benefits attributable to the use of Marine Highway services do not factor into many private sector transportation decisions.

The private sector will ultimately be the key to the success of America's Marine Highway through innovation, outreach, and investment. Private operators must demonstrate to shippers and the public that they can provide highly reliable and cost-effective transportation services by sound management and implementation of the most appropriate technologies for the safe and efficient delivery of cargoes and passengers. They must make efforts to provide greater schedule frequencies and lower the overall cost of service. They must reach out to potential customers, addressing their specific needs and concerns.

Without strong leadership from the Federal government, however, the nation's rivers and coastal waterways will continue to be underutilized for domestic container and trailer freight transportation. It is difficult for private operators to support the scale of investment needed to initiate large scale operations. Private operators are particularly disadvantaged by the fact that many of the important public benefits of water transportation, including congestion reduction, environmental sustainability, and system resiliency, cannot be captured in the form of higher revenues or lower costs to company profits. Government action is required to help overcome these challenges and assist the expansion of Marine Highway services in a significant manner.

With the passage of the Energy Act, Congress set the course for greater Federal government involvement in attaining the national benefits of the America's Marine Highway. The Energy Act established important objectives for MARAD to meet, including the designation of Marine Highway Corridors and Projects, promotion and governmental coordination of development of the Marine Highway, encouragement of the use of America's Marine Highway solutions in State and local planning, establishment of an America's Marine Highway Advisory Board, support for research on Marine Highway (in coordination with EPA), and allowing Marine Highway container and RoRo vessels to qualify for CCF benefits. As discussed in this report, the USDOT and MARAD, in cooperation with the EPA and other agencies, has undertaken numerous actions to comply with these requirements of the Energy Act.

These actions are supported by governmental initiatives that were already underway prior to the Energy Act, including environmental initiatives (e.g., the EPA's SmartWay Transport program), support to maritime industry coalitions, outreach activities including a comprehensive America's Marine Highway website, and effective assistance to startup Marine Highway enterprises. As part of the USDOT and in cooperation with the Department of Commerce, MARAD is strongly committed to supporting the development of a national freight transportation plan that includes a coherent framework to inform State and local planning efforts of the needs and benefits of Marine Highways services.

There are suggestions from the transportation community, described in the last section, which are under consideration by the Administration and thus are not necessarily endorsed by MARAD, USDOT, or the Administration, that stakeholders say could induce increased waterborne freight traffic on

America's Marine Highways. These actions, described in the last section, are as follows:

- Exempt domestic and Great Lakes Saint Lawrence Seaway System movements of non-bulk cargoes from the HMT;
- Equal Customs notification requirements for waterborne container shipments from Canada via the Great Lakes Saint Lawrence Seaway System relative to land-based shipments of the same containers;
- Implement shipper tax credits linked to the value of public benefits associated with the decision to select water transportation. Such credits could be tied to certain routes or areas that have the highest surface congestion or emissions problems;
- Implement investment tax credits and accelerated depreciation for vessel and port equipment purchases, thus reducing the startup and expansion costs for new services;
- Continue appropriations for matching capital grants, including through the recently implemented Marine Highway Grants program and successor programs to the TIGER Discretionary Grants programs (such as a multimodal infrastructure bank). Such grants can be particularly important for smaller operators and ports;
- Modify MARAD's Title XI program to help introduce more environmentally sustainable vessels into the U.S. fleet by giving priority to Marine Highway vessels, granting eligibility to directly-related shoreside facility improvements, and other changes; and
- Establish a Marine Highway infrastructure-oriented program similar to TIFIA that could help to fund port and terminal infrastructure.

Many of these actions could remove important remaining market entry barriers to Marine Highway services. The broad-based tax policy changes, such as establishment of investment tax credits and accelerated depreciation, have the advantages of reducing the risk that government action might convey an unfair advantage to one Marine Highway carrier relative to another. On the other hand, the ability of government to make discretionary awards or offer other types of assistance that affect specific carriers can, if done correctly, help to promote the broader interests of the overall industry and the nation. Grant awards can enable the startup of one or more Marine Highway services in an area where market entry would be advantageous for meeting environmental or other public objectives. Similarly, support for a Marine Highway project that will enable RoRo service using standardized ship design could also foster

80   U.S. Department of Transportation, Maritime Administration

shipbuilding activity, with important employment benefits and national security benefits through enhanced sealift capacity.

In closing, MARAD will use its current authorities, as delegated by the Secretary, and any new authorities granted by Congress in future legislation, to incorporate America's Marine Highway more completely into the national transportation system as a significant provider of efficient and environmentally sound services. In this role, MARAD will fund research and study the commercial market for Marine Highway services, as well as evaluate the outcomes of Marine Highway projects already underway, to verify the value of future Federal investments in this system. Finally, MARAD will work closely with its sister operating administrations at USDOT, other U.S. government agencies including EPA, State and local governments, planning organizations, Marine Highway service operators and other private industry representatives, and the public to insure the success of this important initiative.

APPENDIX: ENERGY INDEPENDENCE AND SECURITY ACT

PUBLIC LAW 110-140 – DEC. 19, 2007
Title XI – Energy Transportation and Infrastructure
Subtitle C—Marine Transportation

[121 STAT. 1760   PUBLIC LAW 110-140 – DEC. 19, 2007]

Subtitle C – Marine Transportation
SEC. 1121. SHORT SEA TRANSPORTATION INITIATIVE.
(a) IN GENERAL. —Title 46, United States Code, is amended by adding after chapter 555 the following:
"CHAPTER 556—SHORT SEA TRANSPORTATION
"Sec. 55601. Short sea transportation program. "Sec. 55602. Cargo and shippers.
"Sec. 55603. Interagency coordination.
"Sec. 55604. Research on short sea transportation. "Sec. 55605. Short sea transportation defined.
"§ 55601. Short sea transportation program
ESTABLISHMENT.—The Secretary of Transportation shall establish a short sea transportation program and designate short sea transportation projects to be conducted under the program to mitigate landside congestion.

PROGRAM ELEMENTS.—The program shall encourage the use of short sea transportation through the development and expansion of—

(1) documented vessels;

(2) shipper utilization;

(3) port and landside infrastructure; and

(4) marine transportation strategies by State and local governments.

Designation

"(c) SHORT SEA TRANSPORTATION ROUTES.—The Secretary shall designate short sea transportation routes as extensions of the surface transportation system to focus public and private efforts to use the waterways to relieve landside congestion along coastal corridors. The Secretary may collect and disseminate data for the designation and delineation of short sea transportation routes.

"(d) PROJECT DESIGNATION.—The Secretary may designate a project to be a short sea transportation project if the Secretary determines that the project may—

(1) offer a waterborne alternative to available landside transportation services using documented vessels; and

(2) provide transportation services for passengers or freight (or both) that may reduce congestion on landside infrastructure using documented vessels.

"(e) ELEMENTS OF PROGRAM. —For a short sea transportation project designated under this section, the Secretary may—

(1) promote the development of short sea transportation services;

(2) coordinate, with ports, State departments of transportation, localities, other public agencies, and the private sector and on the development of landside facilities and infrastructure to support short sea transportation services; and

(3) develop performance measures for the short sea transportation program.

"(f) MULTISTATE, STATE AND REGIONAL TRANSPORTATION PLANNING. —The Secretary, in consultation with Federal entities and State and local governments, shall develop strategies to encourage the use of short sea transportation for transportation of passengers and cargo. The Secretary shall—

[Page 121 STAT. 1761]

82 U.S. Department of Transportation, Maritime Administration

(1) assess the extent to which States and local governments include short sea transportation and other marine transportation solutions in their transportation planning;

(2) encourage State departments of transportation to develop strategies, where appropriate, to incorporate short sea transportation, ferries, and other marine transportation solutions for regional and interstate transport of freight and passengers in their transportation planning; and

(3) encourage groups of States and multi-State transportation entities to determine how short sea transportation can address congestion, bottlenecks, and other interstate transportation challenges.

"§ 55602. Cargo and shippers

(a) MEMORANDUMS OF AGREEMENT.—The Secretary of Transportation shall enter into memorandums of understanding with the heads of other Federal entities to transport federally owned or generated cargo using a short sea transportation project designated under section 55601 when practical or available.

(b) SHORT-TERM INCENTIVES.—The Secretary shall consult shippers and other participants in transportation logistics and develop proposals for short-term incentives to encourage the use of short sea transportation.

"§ 55603. Interagency coordination Establishment.

"The Secretary of Transportation shall establish a board to identify and seek solutions to impediments hindering effective use of short sea transportation. The board shall include representatives of the Environmental Protection Agency and other Federal, State, and local governmental entities and private sector entities.

"§55604. Research on short sea transportation

"The Secretary of Transportation, in consultation with the Administrator of the Environmental Protection Agency, may conduct research on short sea transportation, regarding—

(1) the environmental and transportation benefits to be derived from short sea transportation alternatives for other forms of transportation;

(2) technology, vessel design, and other improvements that would reduce emissions, increase fuel economy, and lower costs of short sea transportation and increase the efficiency of inter-modal transfers; and

(3) solutions to impediments to short sea transportation projects designated under section 55601.

"§55605. Short sea transportation defined

"In this chapter, the term 'short sea transportation' means the carriage by vessel of cargo—

"(1) that is—

(A) contained in intermodal cargo containers and loaded by crane on the vessel; or

(B) loaded on the vessel by means of wheeled technology; and

"(2) that is—

(A) loaded at a port in the United States and unloaded either at another port in the United States or at a port

[Page 121 STAT. 1762]

in Canada located in the Great Lakes Saint Lawrence Seaway System; or

(B) loaded at a port in Canada located in the Great Lakes Saint Lawrence Seaway System and unloaded at a port in the United States.".

(b) CLERICAL AMENDMENT. —The table of chapters at the beginning of subtitle V of such title is amended by inserting after the item relating to chapter 555 the following:

Deadlines. 46 USC 55601 note.

"556. Short Sea Transportation   55601".

(c) REGULATIONS.—

(1) INTERIM REGULATIONS. —Not later than 90 days after the date of enactment of this Act, the Secretary of Transportation shall issue temporary regulations to implement the program under this section. Subchapter II of chapter 5 of title 5, United States Code, does not apply to a temporary regulation issued under this paragraph or to an amendment to such a temporary regulation.

(2) FINAL REGULATIONS. —Not later than October 1, 2008, the Secretary of Transportation shall issue final regulations to implement the program under this section.

SEC. 1122. SHORT SEA SHIPPING ELIGIBILITY FOR CAPITAL CONSTRUCTION FUND.

(a) DEFINITION OF QUALIFIED VESSEL.—Section 53501 of title 46, United States Code, is amended—

(1) in paragraph (5)(A)(iii) by striking "or noncontiguous domestic" and inserting "noncontiguous domestic, or short sea transportation trade"; and

(2) by inserting after paragraph (6) the following:

"(7) SHORT SEA TRANSPORTATION TRADE. —The term 'short sea transportation trade' means the carriage by vessel of cargo—

"(A) that is—

84   U.S. Department of Transportation, Maritime Administration

(i) contained in intermodal cargo containers and loaded by crane on the vessel; or

(ii) loaded on the vessel by means of wheeled technology; and

"(B) that is—

(i) loaded at a port in the United States and unloaded either at another port in the United States or at a port in Canada located in the Great Lakes Saint Lawrence Seaway System; or

(ii) loaded at a port in Canada located in the Great Lakes Saint Lawrence Seaway System and unloaded at a port in the United States.".

(b) ALLOWABLE PURPOSE.—Section 53503(b) of such title is amended by striking "or noncontiguous domestic trade" and inserting "noncontiguous domestic, or short sea transportation trade".

SEC. 1123. SHORT SEA TRANSPORTATION REPORT.

Not later than 1 year after the date of enactment of this

Act, the Secretary of Transportation, in consultation with the Administrator of the Environmental Protection Agency, shall submit to the Committee on Transportation and Infrastructure of the House of Representatives and the Committee on Commerce, Science, and

[Page 121 STAT. 1763]

Transportation of the Senate a report on the short sea transportation program established under the amendments made by section 1121. The report shall include a description of the activities conducted under the program, and any recommendations for further legislative or administrative action that the Secretary of Transportation considers appropriate.

End Notes

[1] A ton-mile is a physical measure of freight transportation output, defined as one ton of freight shipped one mile. It therefore reflects both the volume shipped (tons) and the distance shipped (miles).

[2] With regard to freight, the Energy Act specifically defines short sea shipping to mean "the carriage by vessel of cargo – (1) that is (A) contained in intermodal cargo containers and loaded by crane on the vessel; or (B) loaded on the vessel by means of wheeled technology...", the latter of which largely consists of highway trailers.

[3] The shift to landside transportation modes from water transportation is attributable to a range of factors too complicated to discuss adequately in this report, including (but not limited to) the completion of the Interstate Highway System, use of larger and more specialized trucks and train cars, deregulation of motor carriers and railroads, changing technologies and logistics practices, and the implementation of pipeline capacity for petroleum transport. A critical factor contributing to the shift – the inability of markets to fully capture social costs

and benefits associated with the use of different transportation modes – is described in this chapter.

[4] U.S. Department of Transportation, Research and Innovative Technology Administration, Bureau of Transportation Statistics, National Transportation Statistics 2010, http://www.bts.gov/publications/national_transportation_statistics/pdf/entire.pdf; Table 1-46a (U.S. Ton-Miles of Freight (Millions)), supplemented with 2007 intercity truck ton-miles from Table 1-46b (U.S. Ton-Miles of Freight (BTS Special Tabulation) (Millions)); and Table 1-50 (U.S. Waterborne Freight (Million short tons)). Note that the Federal Highway Administration has alternative estimates of truck ton-miles that are significantly higher than those reported by the BTS; a consistent series of these numbers might show that water transportation has had lower shares of the domestic freight transportation market than reported above.

[5] U.S. Department of Transportation, Federal Highway Administration, Office of Freight Management and Operations, Freight Facts and Figures 2009, November 2009; Table 2-1 (Weight of Shipments by Transportation Mode: 2002, 2008, and 2035 (millions of tons)), p. 11.

[6] Ibid, p. 11.

[7] U.S. Department of Energy, Energy Information Administration, Annual Energy Outlook 2010 With Projections to 2035, DOE/EIA-0383(2010), April 2010,Table A7 (Transportation Sector Key Indicators and Delivered Energy Consumption: Energy Use by Mode (quadrillion Btu)), p. 122.

[8] Ibid, Table A19 (Energy-Related Carbon Dioxide Emissions by End Use: Transportation (Million Metric Tons)), p. 144.

[9] "Presidential Memorandum Regarding Fuel Efficiency Standards," White House, May 21, 2010; also, National Highway Traffic Safety Administration, U.S. Department of Transportation, "Notice of Intent to Prepare an Environmental Impact Statement for New Medium- and Heavy-Duty Fuel Efficiency Improvement Program," 75 FR 33565 (June 14, 2010).

[10] One TEU (twenty-foot equivalent unit) represents the cargo capacity of a standard intermodal container, 20 feet (6.1 m) long and 8 feet (2.4 m) wide. Actual shipping containers vary in size but can be expressed in term of TEU; for instance, a 40 foot long container would be equivalent to two TEU.

[11] U.S. Army Corps of Engineers, Waterborne Commerce Statistics Center, "2008 Waterborne Container Traffic for U.S. Ports and all 50 States and U.S. Territories by Port TEU" (http://www.iwr.usace.army.mil/ndc/wcsc/wcsc.htm) and Waterborne Commerce of the United States, detailed files, 2008.

[12] Intermodal Association of America, "Intermodal Industry Statistics, Year 2008 Industry Statistics – Rail Intermodal Traffic Activity" (http://www.intermodal.org/statistics_files /stats2.shtml).

[13] Users of the surface transportation system pay a variety of taxes and fees which, depending on how these payments are allocated, may partially reimburse some of the external costs discussed in this report. For instance, fuel taxes may reimburse infrastructure maintenance costs for certain classes of users. Private insurance premiums cover some percentage of the full social costs of crashes. It would be impractical to adequately describe the topic of cost reimbursement in this report, although the external costs and benefits described in this report are generally believed to be undervalued or ignored in private sector transportation investment and use decisions. In January 2011, the Government Accountability Office (GAO) issued the report, Surface Freight Transportation: A Comparison of the Costs of

Road, Rail, and Waterways Freight Shipments That Are Not Passed on to Consumers (GAO-11-134). The GAO report provides an assessment of the external costs of surface freight transportation and the degree to which these costs are reimbursed by the prices and taxes charged to users for each transportation mode. Among its findings is that waterways transportation has the smallest amount of unreimbursed external costs per million ton-miles of freight moved (Table 3, pp. 22-23).

[14] To the extent that use of a Marine Highway service reduces the unreimbursed external costs caused by competing transportation modes, this can be viewed as a benefit associated with the use of the Marine Highway service.

[15] Energy Independence and Security Act of 2007 (Pub.L. 110-140), Title XI – Energy Transportation and Infrastructure, Subtitle C – Marine Transportation; Sec. 1121 – Short Sea Transportation Initiative.

[16] See Statement of William O. Gray in Committee for a Study of the Federal Role in the Marine Transportation System, The Marine Transportation System and the Federal Role: Measuring Performance, Targeting Improvement, Transportation Research Board, Special Report 279, Washington DC, 2004, pp. 156-165.

[17] See, for instance, European Commission, Actions Listed in the On-Going Action Plan for the Promotion of Short Sea Shipping, 17 March 2009, at http://ec.europa.eu/transport/maritime /doc/sss_2009_list_of_actions.pdf.

[18] Unless otherwise noted, statistics in this paragraph on European container barge activity are from Rob Konings and Hugo Priemus, "Terminals and the Competitiveness of Container Barge Transport," Ports and Waterways, Transportation Research Board, Transportation Research Record No. 2062, 2008, p. 39.

[19] The vitality of short sea shipping in Europe is well-documented. See, for instance, the newsletter "Aboard!" by the Shortsea Promotion Center Flanders, No. 34, October 2009, at http://www.shortsea.be/html_en/nieuws/documents/SSSNB34_ENG.pdf.

[20] European Commission, "Maritime transport: What do we want to achieve?" at http://ec.europa.eu/transport/maritime/index_en.htm.

[21] Government Accountability Office, Freight Transportation: Short Sea Shipping Option Shows Importance of Systematic Approach to Public Investment Decisions, GAO-05-768, July 2005, p. 8.

[22] National Surface Transportation Policy and Revenue Study Commission, Transportation for Tomorrow, Volume 1, December 2007, p. 2.

[23] U.S. Department of Transportation, Federal Highway Administration, Office of Freight Management and Operations, Freight Facts and Figures 2009, November 2009, Table 2-1 (Weight of Shipments by Transportation Mode: 2002, 2008, and 2035 (millions of tons)), p.11.

[24] U.S. Department of Transportation, Research and Innovative Technology Administration, Bureau of Transportation Statistics, National Transportation Statistics 2010; http://www.bts.gov/publications/national_transportation_statistics/pdf/entire.pdf; Table 1-37 (U.S. Passenger-Miles (Millions)).

[25] Committee for the Study of Funding Options for Freight Transportation Projects of National Significance, Funding Options for Freight Transportation Projects, Transportation Research Board, Special Report 297, Washington DC, 2009, p. 11.

[26] Global Insight with Reeve & Associates, Four Corridor Case Studies of Short-Sea Shipping Services: Short-Sea Shipping Business Case Analysis, submitted to the U.S. Department of Transportation Office of the Secretary/Maritime Administration, Ref. #DTOS59-04-Q-00069, Washington, DC, August 15, 2006, pp. 15-16.

[27] European short sea container services have been found to be increasingly competitive on distances of less than 500 kilometers (311 miles) (see Rob Konings and Hugo Priemus, "Terminals and the Competitiveness of Container Barge Transport," Ports and Waterways, Transportation Research Board, Transportation Research Record No. 2062, 2008, p. 44).

[28] U.S. Department of Labor, Bureau of Labor Statistics, Occupational Outlook Handbook, 2010-11 Edition, Transportation and Material Moving Occupations, Water Transportation Occupations, at http://www.bls.gov/oco/ocos247.htm.

[29] U.S. Department of Transportation, Maritime Administration, "U.S. Water Transportation Statistical Snapshot," July 2009, (U.S. Employment in Water Transportation and Related Industries, 2003-2008), p. 19, based on data from the U.S. Bureau of Labor Statistics, Current Employment Statistics Survey.

[30] Ibid, (U.S. Water Transportation Gross Output, 2002-2007), p. 21, based on data from the U.S. Bureau of Economic Analysis, Gross Domestic Product by Industry Accounts.

[31] 46 CFR §12.02-7. Individuals navigating rivers exclusively and the smaller inland lakes, below the rank of licensed officer and registered staff officer, are exempt from this requirement.

[32] 46 CFR § 15.401.

[33] MARAD operates the U.S. Merchant Marine Academy at Kings Point, NY. MARAD also provides training vessels and other support to the six State maritime academies, which are in Texas, California, New York, Michigan, Maine, and Massachusetts. These academies provide four-year undergraduate programs and their graduates qualify for unlimited horsepower/tonnage license endorsements to their USCG MMC. Their graduates find employment as licensed mariners and in shoreside occupations such as shipyard management and transportation logistics.

[34] Participating schools are Ballard Marine Academy, Seattle, WA; Banning High School, Wilmington, CA; Dixon High School – Marine Technology Academy, Holly Ridge, NC; Grant Maritime Technologies High School, Sacramento, CA; Harbor High School, Aberdeen, WA; Mar Vista High School, Imperial Beach, CA; Marine Academy of Science and Technology, Highlands, NJ; Marine Academy of Technology and Environmental Science, Manahawkin, NJ; Maritime Academy Charter School, Philadelphia, PA; Maritime Industries Academy High School, Baltimore, MD; Maritime Science and Technology High School, Miami, FL; New Orleans Maritime High School, New Orleans, LA; New York Harbor School, Brooklyn, NY; Port of Los Angeles High School, San Pedro, CA; Riviera Beach Maritime Academy, Riviera Beach, FL; South Broward High School, Hollywood, FL; Sumner Memorial High School, Sullivan, ME; The Maritime Academy of Toledo, Toledo, OH; and Western New York Maritime Charter School, Buffalo, NY.

[35] The estimate of shipyard job years is based on 1,251,000 labor hours (assuming 2,080 labor hours per job year) to build a RoRo/containership with a total lightship weight of 14,400 metric tons. The labor hour estimate, current as of August 20, 2010, was prepared by Spar Associates, Inc. in Appendix A of the Multi-purpose American Marine Highways Series Production Ship Task 7.4 Final Report, October 12, 2010.

[36] U.S. Department of Transportation, Research and Innovative Technology Administration, Bureau of Transportation Statistics, National Transportation Statistics 2010, http://www.bts.gov/publications/national_transportation_statistics/pdf/entire.pdf; Table 1-1 (System Mileage Within the United States (Statute miles)). Statistics are for 2007.

[37] Ibid, Table 1-32 (U.S. Vehicle-Miles (Millions)).

[38] Texas Transportation Institute, 2009 Urban Mobility Report, Texas Transportation Institute, 2009, p.1.

88   U.S. Department of Transportation, Maritime Administration

[39] U.S. Department of Transportation, Federal Highway Administration, Office of Freight Management and Operations, Freight Facts and Figures 2009, November 2009, p. 33.

[40] "Chicago rail projects getting a $100 million federal boost," Chicago Tribune, February 18, 2010. The article reports that, "The federal [TIGER] grant, being announced Wednesday, will be used to fund the 16 rail projects under the Chicago Region Environmental and Transportation Efficiency program, CREATE. It's intended to unclog bottlenecks that cause freight trains to take a day or longer to pass through Chicago and block passenger trains and vehicles."

[41] Government Accountability Office, Freight Transportation: Strategies Needed to Address Planning and Financing Limitations, GAO-04-165, December 2003, Highlights.

[42] U.S. Department of Transportation, Federal Highway Administration, Addendum to the 1997 Federal Highway Cost Allocation Study Final Report, May 2000, Table 13 (2000 Pavement, Congestion, Crash, Air Pollution, and Noise Costs for Illustrative Vehicles Under Specific Conditions) and "Summary and Conclusions."

[43] IHS Global Insight, "An Inland Port or an Intermodal Center?," February 26, 2010.

[44] Institute for Global Maritime Studies in cooperation with The Fletcher School of Law and Diplomacy, America's Deep Blue Highway: How Coastal Shipping Could Reduce Traffic Congestion, Lower Pollution, And Bolster National Security, Tufts University, September 2008, p. 88.

[45] This estimate does not include the costs of acquiring vessels to serve the loop service. Vessel costs would be borne by the private operator of the loop service, however, just as private operators bear truck and train equipment costs on landside transportation routes.

[46] I-95 Corridor Coalition, A 2040 Vision for the I-95 Coalition Region, Supporting Economic Growth in a Carbon-Constrained Environment, Executive Summary, December 2008.

[47] U.S. Department of Transportation, Federal Highway Administration, Addendum to the 1997 Federal Highway Cost Allocation Study Final Report, May 2000, Table 13 (2000 Pavement, Congestion, Crash, Air Pollution, and Noise Costs for Illustrative Vehicles Under Specific Conditions) and "Summary and Conclusions."

[48] Federal commercial vehicle maximum standards on the Interstate Highway System (IHS) are: Single Axle, 20,000 pounds; Tandem Axle, 34,000 pounds; and Gross Vehicle Weight, 80,000 pounds. Federal weight limits also apply to bridges on the IHS as specified in the Bridge Formula. Federal law includes provisions, exemptions, and variations applicable to particular States, routes, vehicles, or operations that allow heavier trucks to operate. FHWA policy is that each State should enforce vehicle size and weight laws to assure that violations are discouraged and vehicles traversing the highway system do not exceed the limits specified by law. The thoroughness of enforcement of weight laws can vary significantly among States (less than 1 percent of the trucks are weighed at some ports-of-entry) and some studies have indicated that overweight trucks are not uncommon on the interstate highways of some States (see Arizona Transportation Research Center, Estimating the Cost of Overweight Vehicle Travel on Arizona Highways, Arizona Department of Transportation, Project 528, January 2006). Unfortunately, hard data on overweight vehicles are lacking and inconsistent, with the range of estimates for the percentage of vehicles that are overweight ranging from less than one-half of one-percent to a high of 30 percent (Ibid). Federal restrictions do not apply to State highways, although States individually establish their own weight limits for these roads.

[49] U.S. Department of Transportation, Federal Highway Administration, Comprehensive Truck Size and Weight Study, Volume 1, Summary Report, August 2000, pp. ES-10-11.

[50] Hanson Professional Services, Inc., Business Perspectives on the Feasibility of Container-on-Barge Service: Alabama Freight Mobility Study Phase 1, prepared for the Coalition of Alabama Waterways Associations, April 9, 2007, p. 48.

[51] U.S. Department of Energy, Energy Information Administration, Annual Energy Outlook 2010 With Projections to 2035, DOE/EIA-0383(2010), April 2010, pp. 63 and 75.

[52] Ibid, Table A7, (Transportation Sector Key Indicators and Delivered Energy Consumption: Energy Use by Mode (quadrillion Btu)), p. 122.

[53] Ibid, Table 11 (Projections of energy consumption by sector, 2007-2035), p. 87.

[54] "Presidential Memorandum Regarding Fuel Efficiency Standards," White House, May 21, 2010. As noted in the memorandum, preliminary estimates indicate that large tractor trailers can improve fuel efficiency by as much as 25 percent with the use of existing technologies.

[55] A BTU is a British Thermal Unit which is a unit of energy equal to about 1.06 kilojoules. The conversion of ton-miles per gallon of diesel fuel to BTUs per ton-mile is based on 130,500 BTU per gallon of diesel fuel. [56]Texas Transportation Institute, Center for Ports and Waterways, A Modal Comparison of Domestic Freight Transportation Effects on the General Public, prepared for the U.S. Department of Transportation, Maritime Administration, and National Waterways Foundation, December 2007, p. 42.

[57] As measured in carbon output (which correlates closely to fuel efficiency for the petroleum fuels currently used in freight transportation), the fuel efficiency of oceangoing ships compares favorably to land-based freight modes (see International Maritime Organization, Report MEPC 59/INF.10 ANNEX, April 9, 2009, "Prevention of Air Pollution from Ships, Second IMO GHG Study 2009," pp. 174-177). Liquid and dry bulk oceangoing vessels of more than 20,000 deadweight tons capacity can carry a ton of cargo two or more times as far as the next most fuel-efficient modal alternative, although such vessels are larger than would be used for Marine Highway applications.

[58] A recently released study by the Federal Railroad Administration (FRA), Comparative Evaluation of Rail and Truck Fuel Efficiency on Competitive Corridors, found that distance, route and, type of traffic affect fuel efficiency. The study found that railroads can get up to 512 ton-miles per gallon (255 BTU per ton-mile) when assessing comparative truck offerings between the modes over the same corridor and transporting the same commodity. The study was prepared for FRA by ICF International and was released in November 2009.

[59] U.S. Department of Transportation, Federal Highway Administration, Office of Freight Management and Operations, Freight Facts and Figures 2009, November 2009, p. 26.

[60] As discussed previously, public benefits associated with water transportation, including reduced national dependence on imported oil, improved public safety and security, reduced greenhouse gases, and other social impacts will typically not affect decisions by private shippers because these benefits are not captured directly by the shipper in the form of revenues or cost savings.

[61] U.S. Department of Energy, Energy Information Administration, Annual Energy Outlook 2010 With Projections to 2035, DOE/EIA-0383(2010), April 2010, Table A19 (Energy-Related Carbon Dioxide Emissions by End Use: Transportation (Million Metric Tons)), p. 144.

[62] 49 U.S.C. § 32902(k)(2).

[63] U.S. Department of Transportation, National Highway Traffic Safety Administration, "Notice of Intent to Prepare an Environmental Impact Statement for New Medium- and Heavy-Duty Fuel Efficiency Improvement Program," 75 FR 33565 (June 14, 2010).

[64] International Maritime Organization, Report MEPC 59/INF.10 ANNEX, April 9, 2009, "Prevention of Air Pollution from Ships, Second IMO GHG Study 2009," pp. 174-177.

90 U.S. Department of Transportation, Maritime Administration

Information in Tables 9-1 through 9-3 has been converted from tonne/kilometer units to ton/mile equivalents.

[65] Texas Transportation Institute, Center for Ports and Waterways, A Modal Comparison of Domestic Freight Transportation Effects on the General Public, prepared for the U.S. Department of Transportation, Maritime Administration, and National Waterways Foundation, December 2007, p. 38.

[66] Environmental Protection Agency, "Nonroad Engines, Equipment, and Vehicles: Diesel Boats and Ships" website at http://www.epa.gov/otaq/marine.htm#regs.

[67] Environmental Protection Agency, "Control of Emissions of Air Pollution from Locomotives and Marine Compression-Ignition Engines Less Than 30 Liters per Cylinder," 73 FR 37096 (June 30, 2008).

[68] Environmental Protection Agency, "Nonroad Engines, Equipment, and Vehicles: Ocean-going Vessels," 73 FR 22896 (April 30, 2010).

[69] Environmental Protection Agency News Release, "EPA Strengthens Smog Standard/Proposed standards, strictest to date, will protect the health of all Americans, especially children," January 7, 2010.

[70] Many coastal vessels (including tugs) operating in Marine Highway service are or will be greater than 200 gross register tons (Domestic Tonnage – a measure of internal volume) or 500 gross tons (International Tonnage Convention), operating seaward of the boundary lines specified in Title 46 CFR Part 7 and hence are subject to international Standards of Training, Certification, and Watchkeeping (STCW). The unlicensed mariners aboard these vessels will have the same qualifications as those necessary to crew sealift surge vessels. The size and horsepower of the vessels will determine the necessary qualification of the officers. Although these vessels may not require officers with deep sea qualifications, an increasing number of maritime academy graduates are crewing these vessels and are a part of the pool of officers we depend on to crew sealift surge vessels.

[71] Separately from the USDOT, the DOD's Military Sealift Command (MSC) operates a Sealift Program that provides high-quality ocean transportation for the Department of Defense and other Federal agencies during peacetime and war. The program manages a mix of government-owned and long-term-chartered dry cargo ships and tankers, as well as additional short-term or voyage-chartered ships. Among the 18 sealift vessels owned by the MSC are 11 large, medium-speed RoRo ships.

[72] U.S. Department of Transportation, Maritime Administration, The Maritime Administration and the U.S. Marine Transportation System: A Vision for the 21st Century, November 2007, p. 30.

[73] U.S. Department of Transportation, Maritime Administration, "Budget Estimates Fiscal Year 2009: Maritime Administration," p. 105.

[74] A description of the types of vessels that are or could be employed in Marine Highway services is provided in C. James Kruse and Nathan Hutson, North American Marine Highways, Transportation Research Board, National Cooperative Freight Research Program, NCFRP Report 5, Washington DC, 2010, pp. 13-18

[75] U.S. Department of Commerce, Bureau of Export Administration, National Security Assessment of the U.S. Shipbuilding and Repair Industry, (003-009-00719-4) May 2001.

[76] John Malone and Matthew P. Tedesco, NSRP Short Sea Shipping Roadmap, September 30, 2007, p. 8. Note that U.S. shipyards annually build large numbers of tugs, barges, offshore service vessels, crew boats, utility boats, and other small vessels. The emphasis above concerns larger, militarily-useful self-propelled vessels.

[77] U.S. Department of Labor, Bureau of Labor Statistics, Current Employment Statistics Survey.

[78] U.S. Department of Transportation, Research and Innovative Technology Administration, Bureau of Transportation Statistics, National Transportation Statistics 2010; http://www.bts.gov/publications/national_transportation_statistics/pdf/entire.pdf; Transit Profile, Performance, Passenger-Miles, Ferryboat, p. 419 of 500. Also see next footnote.

[79] Ibid, Table 2-33a (Transit Safety Data by Mode for All Reported Incidents), footnote a. Fatality data are combined for cable cars, inclined planes, jitneys, and ferry boats, with no one year showing more than two fatalities collectively for these modes, except for 2003 with 11 of the 12 fatalities in that year attributable to the Staten Island Ferry incident. Note that the Staten Island Ferry has experienced other incidents, most recently on May 8, 2010, but without fatalities.

[80] Truck freight ton-mile data are from the Federal Highway Administration Freight Analysis Framework (FAF) version 3 estimate for 2007. There were 4,822 fatalities associated with large truck crashes in 2007 as reported in U.S. Department of Transportation, Federal Motor Carrier Safety Administration, Large Truck and Bus Crash Facts 2008, March 2010; Table 30 (Fatalities in Crashes Involving Large Trucks by State, 1998-2008). This total includes fatalities associated with dump trucks, concrete mixer trucks, and garbage trucks. Note that fatalities associated with crashes of large trucks fell sharply in 2008 to 4,229 but there are no comparable freight ton-mile data for this year.

[81] The 0.47 fatalities per billion ton-miles rate is based on Ibid, Table 1-46b (U.S. Ton-Miles of Freight) and Table 2-35 (Railroad Only and Grade Crossing Fatalities by Victim Class), which reports 849 fatalities in 2007 (fatalities fell from this level in 2008 and 2009). Note that the Federal Railroad Administration (FRA) calculates a fatality rate lower than 0.47 per billion ton-miles of rail freight. Under 49 U.S.C. §20901, all railroads are required to file a report with the Secretary of Transportation on all accidents and incidents resulting in injury or death to an individual or damage to equipment or a roadbed arising from the carrier's operations during the month. FRA compiles these reports for the Secretary. For 2007, the carriers reported 631 fatalities for all freight railroads. Assuming that the 1.819.6 billion railroad freight ton-miles in 2007 reported in the National Transportation Statistics 2010 is accurate (the Surface Transportation Board Carload Waybill Sample shows a higher ton-mile count), the fatality rate for freight railroads would be 0.33 per billion ton-miles of freight.

[82] Data based on Ibid, Table 1-46b (U.S. Ton-Miles of Freight) and Table 2-1 (Transportation Fatalities by Mode, Waterborne Total), including fishing vessels but excluding recreational boating, totaling 126 non-recreational waterborne fatalities in 2007.

[83] Inland marine towing has a slightly lower ratio of large spills (1,000 gallons or more) per million ton-miles than does rail and a significantly lower rate than trucks based on 2000-2004 data as reported in Texas Transportation Institute, Center for Ports and Waterways, A Modal Comparison of Domestic Freight Transportation Effects on the General Public, prepared for the U.S. Department of Transportation, Maritime Administration, and National Waterways Foundation, December 2007, p. 47.

[84] National Transportation Safety Board, Railroad Accident Brief, Accident Number: DCA-01-MR-004, NTSB/RAB-04/08, 2004.

[85] Lewis M. Branscomb, Mark Fagan, Philip Auerswald, Ryan N. Ellis, and Raphael Barcham, Rail Transportation of Toxic Inhalation Hazards: Policy Responses to the Safety and Security Externality, John F. Kennedy School of Government, RPP-2010-01, 2010, pp. 16-23. Other rail incidents described in this report include ones at New Orleans, LA, September 1987 (butadiene), Graniteville, SC, June 2005 (chlorine gas), Macdona, TX, June 2004 (chlorine gas), and Minot, ND, January 2002 (anhydrous ammonia).

86 Ibid, p. 5.

87 Ibid, p. 6.

88 The railroads face huge potential liabilities for which they must self-insure or purchase very expensive insurance. It is generally not possible to obtain insurance for damages above $1 billion. Ibid, p. 65, footnote 190.

89 The referenced report by Branscomb et al., Rail Transportation of Toxic Inhalation Hazards: Policy Responses to the Safety and Security Externality, provides a detailed discussion of benefits that could be realized by the correct pricing of hazmat transportation services.

90 On June 12, 2007, Senator Frank R. Lautenberg introduced the "Maritime Hazardous Cargo Security Act of 2007" (S. 1594) to require the U.S. Department of Homeland Security to improve security for the vessels and facilities that ship and receive particularly dangerous chemicals and petrochemicals. The emphasis of the bill was on ships carrying international cargoes such as liquefied natural gas, but also included chlorine, anhydrous ammonia, and other chemicals.

91 Institute for Global Maritime Studies in cooperation with The Fletcher School of Law and Diplomacy, America's Deep Blue Highway: How Coastal Shipping Could Reduce Traffic Congestion, Lower Pollution, And Bolster National Security, Tufts University, September 2008, pp. 52-80. IGMS conducted a detailed assessment of existing vulnerabilities along several major U.S. coastal highway corridors: I-95 along the east coast; I-5 along the west coast; and the Gulf coast lengths of I-10 and I-75. Using these examples, IGMS identified various points of vulnerability as well as coastal shipping ports and water routes that could be used to circumvent these points in an emergency.

92 "Transit Shatters Records as Bay Bridge Remains Closed," Bay Area Public Transportation Examiner, October 20, 2009 at http://www.examiner.com/x-11025-Bay-Area-Public-Transportation-Examiner~y2009m10d30-Transitshatters-records-as-Bay-Bridge-remains-closed.

93 The Staten Island Ferry website at http://www.siferry.com/. Other information about the role of water and transit transportation in the response to the September 11 attack is provided in a report by Brian Jenkins and Frances Edwards-Winslow, Saving City Lifelines: Lessons Learned in the 9-11 Terrorist Attacks, Mineta Transportation Institute, September 2003.

94 Energy Independence and Security Act of 2007, Pub.L. 110-140 codified at 46 U.S.C. § 55601(a).

95 46 U.S.C. § 55602.

96 46 U.S.C. § 55603.

97 46 U.S.C. § 55604.

98 46 U.S.C. §§ 53501, 53503.

99 Office of the Secretary, U.S. Department of Transportation, "Organization and Delegation of Powers and Duties Delegations to the Maritime Administrator," 73 FR 59538 (October 8, 2008).

100 National Defense Authorization Act for Fiscal Year 2010 (Pub.L. 111-84), Section 3515.

101 Consolidated Appropriations Act of 2010 (Pub.L. 111-117) and House Report 111-366, p. 425.

102 American Recovery and Reinvestment Act of 2009 (Pub.L. 111-5).

103 U.S. Department of Transportation, Maritime Administration, "America's Marine Highway Program," Interim final rule with request for comments, 73 FR 59530 (October 9, 2008); amended by "America's Marine Highway Program, Corrections" Correcting amendment, 73 FR 64885 (October 31, 2008).

America's Marine Highway: Report to Congress   93

[104] U.S. Department of Transportation, Maritime Administration, "America's Marine Highway Program," Final rule, 75 FR 18095 (April 9, 2010).

[105] See U.S. Department of Transportation, Maritime Administration, "America's Marine Highway Program" website at http://www.marad.dot.gov/ships_shipping_landing_page /mhi_home/mhi_home.htm.

[106] Authorized under 46 U.S.C. § 55601(d).

[107] U.S. Department of Transportation, Maritime Administration, "Solicitation of Applications for Marine Highway Projects," 75 FR 19670 (April 15, 2010).

[108] U.S. Department of Transportation, Maritime Administration, "U.S. Transportation Secretary LaHood Announces Corridors, Projects and Initiatives Eligible for Funding as Part of America's Marine Highway" MARAD 13-10, August 11, 2010 at http://www.marad.dot.gov/news_room_landing_page/news_releases_summary/news_releas e/MARAD_13- 10_Marine_highway_Projects_release.htm.

[109] U.S. Department of Transportation, Maritime Administration, "America's Marine Highway Grant Notice of Funding Availability," 75 FR 49017 (August 12, 2010). This notice implements the new grant initiative, authorized under Section 3515 of the National Defense Authorization Act for Fiscal Year 2010. The initial funding for the grants is provided in the "Consolidated Appropriations Act of 2010" (Pub.L. 111-117) which the President signed into law on December 16, 2009.

[110] U.S. Department of Transportation, Maritime Administration, "U.S. Transportation Secretary LaHood Announces $7 Million in Grants to Jumpstart America's Marine Highway Initiative," DOT 176-10, September 20, 2010 at http://www.dot.gov/affairs/2010 /dot17610.html.

[111] See U.S. Department of Transportation, Maritime Administration, "America's Marine Highway Program" website at http://www.marad.dot.gov/ships_shipping_landing_page /mhi_home/mhi_home.htm.

[112] 46 U.S.C. § 55601(e).

[113] 46 U.S.C. § 55601(f).

[114] 46 U.S.C. § 55602(a).

[115] 46 U.S.C. § 55602(b).

[116] 46 U.S.C. § 55603.

[117] 46 U.S.C. § 55604.

[118] 46 U.S.C. §§ 53501, 53503(b).

[119] See EPA web sites: http://www.epa.gov/smartway /and http://www.epa.gov/otaq/diesel /index.htm.

[120] 23 USC § 149 ("The Secretary shall establish and implement a congestion mitigation and air quality improvement program in accordance with this section...."). The Congestion Mitigation and Air Quality (CMAQ) program is jointly administered by FHWA and the Federal Transit Administration to fund projects that reduce criteria air pollutants from transportation-related sources and are based in designated air quality nonattainment or maintenance areas. Accordingly, CMAQ funds can be used by State, regional authorities, and MPOs for water transportation projects that meet these eligibility requirements (such as the new container-on-barge service between Richmond and Norfolk, VA). More information on the CMAQ program is available at http://www.law.cornell.edu/uscode /uscode23/usc_sec_23_00000149----000-.html.

[121] The Marine Highways Cooperative was established on October 15, 2003 and consists of government, academic and private organizations and companies, including MARAD, committed to improving transportation mobility through international and national Marine

94   U.S. Department of Transportation, Maritime Administration

Highway shipping and the development of intermodal coastal and inland trades; more information can be found at www.marinehighways.org.

[122] U.S. Department of Transportation, Maritime Administration, "America's Marine Highway Program" website at http://marad.dot.gov/ships shipping landing page/mhi home/mhi home.htm

[123] Data on emissions and fuel consumption were developed by the Richmond Area MPO and confirmed in two e-mails to the Maritime Administration for this report. These data were developed as part of the MPO's evaluation process before CMAQ funds were awarded to the "64 Express" project in 2008.

[124] Congress authorized this program as the "Supplemental Discretionary Grants for a National Surface Transportation System" program in Title XI of the American Recovery and Reinvestment Act of 2009 (Pub.L. 111- 5).

[125] U.S. Department of Transportation, Transportation Investment Generating Economic Recovery (TIGER) Grants, February 17, 2010.

[126] U.S. Department of Transportation, Maritime Administration, "Groundbreaking Ceremony Signals Start of 'Green' Marine Highway Project" DOT 191-10, October 26, 2010, at http://www.marad.dot.gov/news_room_landing_page/news_releases_summary/news_releas e/DOT_191- 10_news_release.htm.

[127] Environmental Defense Fund, The Good Haul: Innovations that Improve Freight Transportation and Protect the Environment, 2010, pp. 24-25.

[128] Ibid.

[129] Many of the impediments discussed in this report section, as well as additional impediments cited by some members of the water transportation industry, are discussed in C. James Kruse and Nathan Hutson, North American Marine Highways, Transportation Research Board, National Cooperative Freight Research Program, NCFRP Report 5, Washington DC, 2010.

[130] Rob Konings and Hugo Priemus, "Terminals and the Competitiveness of Container Barge Transport," Ports and Waterways, Transportation Research Board, Transportation Research Record No. 2062, 2008, p. 42.

[131] Ibid, p. 42.

[132] Title 10 United States Code, Subtitle A, Part IV, Chapter 131, § 2218.

[133] Stevedoring is the process of loading or unloading the cargo of a ship in port.

[134] Drayage is the transporting of freight short distances by truck to or from the port as part of an overall trip.

[135] Pilotage is the compensation paid to a licensed ship's pilot, who is the person qualified to conduct a ship into and out of a port or in specified waters.

[136] Global Insight, Four Corridor Case Studies of Short-Sea Shipping Services: Short-Sea Shipping Business Case Analysis, prepared for the U.S. Department of Transportation, Office of the Secretary/Maritime Administration, Ref. #DTOS59-04-Q-00069, August 15, 2006, pp. 10 and 36.

[137] Rob Konings and Hugo Priemus, "Terminals and the Competitiveness of Container Barge Transport," Ports and Waterways, Transportation Research Board, Transportation Research Record No. 2062, 2008, pp. 39-49.

[138] Bridgeport Port Authority, "Barge Feeder Service Update" March 2008 at www.umassd.edu/sustainability/riccio.pdf

[139] C. James Kruse and Nathan Hutson, North American Marine Highways, Transportation Research Board, National Cooperative Freight Research Program, NCFRP Report 5, Washington DC, 2010, p. 16

[140] U.S. Department of Transportation, Maritime Administration, "U.S. Water Transportation Statistical Snapshot," July 2009, (U.S. Privately-Owned Fleets, 2003-2008), p. 15 and (U.S.-Flag Privately-Owned Ocean and Great lakes Fleets, 2003-2008), p.17.

[141] Government Accountability Office, Freight Transportation: Short Sea Shipping Option Shows Importance of Systematic Approach to Public Investment Decisions, GAO-05-768, July 2005, pp. 22-23. Tug-and-barge units are significantly less expensive than most self-propelled vessels. U.S. shipyards are able to take advantage of scale economies in the production of tug-and-barge units.

[142] Ibid.

[143] C. James Kruse and Nathan Hutson, North American Marine Highways, Transportation Research Board, National Cooperative Freight Research Program, NCFRP Report 5, Washington DC, 2010, pp. 68, 84.

[144] Hanson Professional Services, Inc., Business Perspectives on the Feasibility of Container-on-Barge Service: Alabama Freight Mobility Study Phase 1, prepared for the Coalition of Alabama Waterways Associations, April 9, 2007, p. 39.

[145] John J. Coyle et al., Supply Chain Management: A Logistics Perspective, Edition: 8, Cengage Learning, Inc., 2009 pp. 343-344.

[146] Hanson Professional Services, Inc., Business Perspectives on the Feasibility of Container-on-Barge Service: Alabama Freight Mobility Study Phase 1, prepared for the Coalition of Alabama Waterways Associations, April 9, 2007, pp. 56-64.

[147] The Volpe Center, Assessment of Short-Sea Shipping Options for Domestic Applications, prepared for Office of Naval Research, December 23, 2009, pp. 76-77.

[148] In some Marine Highway business models, these value added services would be provided by the trucking, rail, and intermodal service providers to which the Marine Highway firm would market line haul marine services.

[149] Rob Konings and Hugo Priemus, "Terminals and the Competitiveness of Container Barge Transport," Ports and Waterways, Transportation Research Board, Transportation Research Record No. 2062, 2008, pp. 39-49. This article has many useful suggestions for promoting short sea shipping.

[150] European Commission, Mobility & Transport, "Short Sea Shipping" at http://ec.europa.eu/transport/maritime/short sea shipping en.htm.

[151] The Government Accountability Office reached similar conclusions with regard to regional and local planning. In its "Highlights" for Freight Transportation: Strategies Needed to Address Planning and Financing Limitations, GAO-04-165, December 2003, Highlights, the GAO notes that "Stakeholders encounter two main limitations in addressing freight mobility challenges. The first relates to the limited visibility that freight projects receive in the process for planning and prioritizing how transportation dollars should be spent. The planning process often lacks a comprehensive evaluation approach, such as a cost-benefit framework that might result in the implementation of freight improvements to better ensure that systemwide, multimodal solutions are considered and adopted where appropriate. The second relates to limitations of federal funding programs, which tend to dedicate funds to a single mode of transportation or a nonfreight purpose."

[152] Some MPOs, however, are in the forefront of Marine Highway planning, such as in the case of the "64 Express" service in Virginia.

[153] Well-known coalitions include the American Association of State and Highway Transportation Officials (AASHTO), the American Public Transportation Association (APTA), the American Trucking Associations (ATA), the Association of American Railroads (AAR), to name a few. Organizations within the maritime community, such as the

American Association of Port Authorities, the Waterways Council, and the American Waterways Operators represent a variety of maritime interests. Only the Marine Highways Cooperative is exclusively focused on the Marine Highway, but is of much lower visibility and operates on a much smaller budget than the others mentioned in this footnote.

[154] Surface transportation service providers chiefly include forwarders, brokers, shipper associations, and third party logistics companies who make actual cargo routing choices.

[155] C. James Kruse and Nathan Hutson, North American Marine Highways, Transportation Research Board, National Cooperative Freight Research Program, NCFRP Report 5, Washington DC, 2010, p. 29. Some Marine Highway movements could involve transshipment through a port and thus more than one charge.

[156] Marine Highway Legislation – 111th Congress at http://www.maritimeadvisors.com/pdf/ MHgrid08052009.pdf. Also, John Frittelli, "Harbor Maintenance Trust Fund Expenditures," Congressional Research Service, January 25, 2010, p. 18. Note that two of these bills would extend HMT exemptions to include cargo shipped to the U.S. from Nova Scotia, which could have significant ramifications for U.S. ports.

[157] Pursuant to Section 343 of the Trade Act of 2002 (Public Law 107-210), U.S. Customs and Border Protection (CBP) published a new regulation in 2003 called the "24 Hour Rule."

[158] David J. Farrell, Jr., "America's Marine Highway a/k/a Short Sea Shipping: A Win-Win Proposition," Benedict's Maritime Bulletin, Third/Fourth Quarter 2007, p. 224.

[159] Government Accountability Office, Freight Transportation: Short Sea Shipping Option Shows Importance of Systematic Approach to Public Investment Decisions, GAO-05-768, July 2005, pp. 14-15. MARAD notes that shippers can experiment with low volume or occasional use of a Marine Highway service without canceling existing truck and railroad contracts to gain experience with the water service.

[160] Investment tax credits have proven to be an excellent vehicle to stimulate growth, including a dramatic surge in the solar energy sector, which saw its market grow by 45 percent within two years of implementing the solar energy investment tax credit (see Solar Energy Industries Association, "Federal Policy Propels U.S. Solar Energy Industry" 2007 at http://www.seia.org/galleries/pdf/Year_in_Review_2007_sm.pdf).

[161] U.S. Department of Transportation, Maritime Administration, "America's Marine Highway Grant Notice of Funding Availability," 75 FR 49017 (August 12, 2010). On October 28, 2009 the President signed the National Defense Authorization Act for Fiscal Year 2010 (Defense Act) (Pub.L. 111-84). Section 3515 of that Act amends Section 55601 of title 46, United States Code by adding a subsection "(g) Grants" that directs the Secretary of Transportation to "establish and implement a short sea transportation grant program to implement projects or components of a project designated under subsection (d)". The grants can fund up to 80 percent of a Marine Highway Project subject to the conditions that the project is financially viable and the operator has shown that "a market exists for the services of the proposed Project as evidenced by contracts or written statements of intent from potential customers."

[162] The Consolidated Appropriations Act of 2010 (Pub.L. 111-117), signed into law by the President on December 16, 2009, appropriates Operating and Training funds to MARAD. Of such funds, up to $7 million is allocated to MARAD's "Secure and Efficient Ports Initiative" through conference report language (House Report 111-366, p. 425).

[163] The Defense Act authorizes the new Port Infrastructure Development Program under Section 3512, to be administered by the Secretary through the Maritime Administrator.

[164] Federal, State, and local agency coordination may shorten timeframes for environmental review. However, the requirements for needed environmental information, assessment, and

America's Marine Highway: Report to Congress

reviews must be maintained and considered up front and integrated into program planning. Environmental protection requirements must be incorporated to assure environmental sustainability.

[165] On February 17, 2009 the President signed the American Recovery and Reinvestment Act of 2009 (Pub.L. 111- 5). Among the provisions of this Act is the creation of the "Supplemental Discretionary Grants for a National Surface Transportation System" program under Title XI, implemented by the Secretary as the "Grants for Transportation Investment Generating Economic Recovery" or "TIGER Discretionary Grants" program. This program extended eligibility for $1.5 billion in TIGER Discretionary Grants to projects in all surface transportation modes and notably to port infrastructure investments, including projects that connect ports to other modes of transportation and improve the efficiency of freight movement. TIGER Discretionary Grants were announced on February 17, 2010 with seven of the 51 grants and a total of $120.44 million awarded to port projects expected to be on Marine Highway Corridors. Other TIGER Discretionary Grant awards benefited rail access to ports.

[166] USDOT was authorized to award $600 million in National Infrastructure Investment Grants pursuant to Title I (Department of Transportation) of the Consolidated Appropriations Act of 2010 (Pub. L. 111-117, Dec. 16, 2009). This appropriation was similar but not identical to the appropriation for the TIGER Discretionary Grant program authorized and implemented pursuant to the Recovery Act. Because of the similarity in program structure and objectives, DOT referred to the grants for National Infrastructure Investments as TIGER II Discretionary Grants. On October 20, 2010, the Secretary announced the award of 42 capital construction projects and 33 planning projects under the TIGER II program. Seven of the 42 capital construction grants and a total of $94.84 million went to port-related projects, some of which will benefit Marine Highway services.

[167] See "FHWA Office of Innovative Program Delivery: TIFIA" web site at http://www.fhwa.dot.gov/ipd/tifia/.

In: America's Marine Highways
Editor: Rafael Pelletier

ISBN: 978-1-62618-857-0
© 2013 Nova Science Publishers, Inc.

Chapter 2

CAN MARINE HIGHWAYS DELIVER?*

John Frittelli

SUMMARY

Policymakers have been discussing the potential for shifting some freight traffic from roads to river and coastal waterways as a means of mitigating highway congestion. While waterways carry substantial amounts of bulk commodities (e.g., grain and coal), seldom are they used to transport containerized cargo (typically finished goods and manufactured parts) between points within the contiguous United States. Trucks, which carry most of this cargo, and railroads, which carry some of it in combination with trucks, offer much faster transit. Yet, at a time when many urban highways are congested, a parallel river or coastal waterway may be little used.

With passage of the Energy Independence and Security Act of 2007 (P.L. 110-140) and the National Defense Authorization Act for FY2010 (P.L. 111-84), Congress moved this idea forward by requiring the Department of Transportation (DOT) to identify waterways that could potentially serve as "marine highways" and providing grant funding for their development. DOT has selected several marine highways for grant funding totaling about $80 million. To be eligible, a marine highway must be an alternative to a congested highway or railroad and be financially viable in a reasonable time frame.

---

* This is an edited, reformatted and augmented version of a Congressional Research Service publication, CRS Report for Congress R41590, from www.crs.gov, prepared for Members and Committees of Congress, dated January 14, 2011.

The prevailing perception is that coastal and river navigation is too slow to attract shippers that utilize trucks and that the additional cargo handling costs at ports negate any potential savings from using waterborne transport. While there are other significant obstacles as well, under highly specific circumstances, marine highways might attract truck freight. Freight corridors characterized by an imbalance in the directional flow of container equipment; shippers with low value, heavy cargoes, and waterside production facilities; and connections with coastal hub ports over medium distances may be suitable for container-on-barge (COB) or coastal shipping services. It also appears that marine highways are more suitable to international rather than domestic shippers because the former have lower service expectations.

A review of the successes and failures of the few marine highway services currently operating in the contiguous United States, as well as those that have failed in the past, indicates that the potential market is limited. In many instances, marine highways have succeeded in capturing only a negligible share of container shipments along a given route. One can question, therefore, whether marine highways will divert enough trucks to provide public benefits commensurate with their costs. Congress may also consider repealing a port use charge, the harbor maintenance tax, for containerized domestic shipments as a means of spurring marine highway development. Repealing the tax raises equity issues because waterway users already benefit from reduced federal user charges compared to trucks, and their other competitor, the railroads, are largely self-financed. The Jones Act is arguably another potential statutory hindrance to marine highway development, particularly coastal highways. This act requires that all domestic shipping be carried in U.S. built ships. Critics claim the act raises the cost of domestic shipping to such a degree that it cannot compete with truck and rail.

BACKGROUND: RECENT FEDERAL SUPPORT

For at least a decade, policymakers have been discussing the potential to shift freight from roads to rivers and coastal waterways as a means of mitigating highway congestion. While U.S. waterways carry substantial amounts of bulk commodities, such as grain, coal, and fuel oil, they are seldom used to transport containerized cargo between points within the lower 48 states. Trucks, which carry most domestic container shipments, and railroads, which carry a large proportion of containers imported or exported by sea, offer much faster transit. Yet, at a time when many highways and rail lines are congested, a parallel river or coastal waterway may be little used.

Can Marine Highways Deliver? 101

With passage of the Energy Independence and Security Act of 2007 (P.L. 110-140, specifically Subtitle C, 121 Stat. 1760), Congress pushed for greater use of marine transportation by requiring the Department of Transportation's (DOT's) Maritime Administration (MARAD) to identify waterways that could potentially serve as "short sea" shipping routes. Subsequently, in the National Defense Authorization Act for FY2010 (P.L. 111-84, specifically section 3515, 123 Stat. 2724), Congress authorized federal grants for financially viable short sea routes covering up to 80% of total project cost. In April 2010, MARAD issued a final rule implementing the program, along with the following explanation:

> In recent years, it has become increasingly evident that the Nation's existing road and rail infrastructure cannot adequately meet our future transportation needs. Land based infrastructure expansion opportunities are limited in many critical bottleneck areas due to geography or very high right-of-way acquisition costs. This is particularly severe in urban areas where there are additional concerns about emissions from transportation sources.[1]

MARAD uses the term "marine highways" instead of "short sea" shipping to convey the purpose of the program, which is to mitigate landside freight bottlenecks. For this reason, projects relating to waterborne shipment of dry and liquid bulk products and oversize cargo too large to fit into a container are not eligible, as these products already move on waterways. Also, freight ferry service to an island without a bridge is ineligible, because no roadway congestion would be relieved. As specified by Congress, shipments to or from Mexico do not qualify, nor do shipments to or from Canada, except those across the Great Lakes.[2] Project eligibility requires a demonstration of public benefits and long-term sustainability without future federal operational support.[3]

DOT has provided grants to several existing or prospective domestic container shipping services, not only under the Marine Highway initiative but also the Transportation Investment Generating Economic Recovery (TIGER) grant program and the Congestion Mitigation Air Quality Improvement Program (CMAQ), as indicated in Table 1.[4] Relative to DOT's total budget, the amount of funding is small and could be viewed as seed money for exploring the feasibility of marine highways. The funding recipients are public entities, and can be states, metropolitan planning organizations, or port authorities, which must find other funding sources to cover a share of a project's total projected cost. These entities are encouraged to develop public/private partnerships with vessel owners and operators, truck and rail carriers, and shippers. These projects represent departures from the federal government's traditional role in domestic marine transportation, which has involved financing navigation infrastructure but generally has not provided vessel operating grants or funds for landside marine terminal infrastructure, such as wharves and cranes.

Table 1. Selected Federal Grant Funding for Marine Highway Projects

Project/Service	Description	Funding Grant(s)	Use of Funds
Stockton and West Sacramento Port Upgrades	Reduce congestion on I-580 between Port of Oakland and Stockton and Sacramento, CA, by shifting truck traffic to container-on-barge (COB) service on deepwater ship channels to these ports.	TIGER I - $30 million	Purchase three cranes and one barge, and construct cargo handling facilities at Stockton and West Sacramento; install onshore power source to reduce ship idling at Oakland.
James River 64 Express	Improve COB service between Port of Norfolk and Richmond, VA, to relieve congestion on I-64 (port truckers also use Route 460 south of the river).	Marine Highway - $1.1 million CMAQ - $2.3 million	Purchase two more barges to increase sailings per week to three.
Tenn-Tom COB	Establish COB service between Port of Mobile, AL, and Itawamba, MS, on the Tenn-Tom waterway.	Marine Highway - $1.76 million	Purchase or modify nine barges for new service.
Cross-Gulf Coastal Service	Improve COB service between Brownsville, TX, and Port Manatee (Tampa), FL.	Marine Highway - $3.34 million TIGER II -$9 million	Modify two barges.
Granite City intermodal river port	Construct a new port at Granite City, IL, (St. Louis area) on the site of a former Army base	TIGER I -$6 million	Construct rail track on port grounds and 10 levee relief wells to protect the port from flooding.

Project/Service	Description	Funding Grant(s)	Use of Funds
	adjacent to the most southern lock (# 27) on the Mississippi River. Not solely targeting container shippers, hopes to attract any kind of shipper.		
Cates Landing intermodal river port	Construct a new port on the Mississippi River in Lake County, northwest Tennessee. Not solely targeting container shippers, hopes to attract any kind of shipper.	TIGER II - $13 million	Construct basic port infrastructure. Land is currently vacant.
Port of Providence Coastal Service	Upgrade container cranes to enable port to handle 1,000 containers per week, relieving congestion on I-95.	TIGER II -$10.5 million	Replace two aged diesel cranes with barge-based electric cranes for handling containers.

Source: U.S. DOT and MARAD press releases, Journal of Commerce articles.

Notes: The Marine Highway initiative also provided $0.8 million in funding to study the feasibility of two West Coast services, two East Coast services, and a COB service at Peoria, IL, on the Illinois waterway. TIGER I was authorized in the American Recovery and Reinvestment Act (P.L. 111-5) under Title XII, providing $1.5 billion in DOT discretionary grants, listing port facilities as eligible recipients; TIGER II was authorized in the FY2010 DOT Appropriations Act (P.L. 111-117). CMAQ is a federal-aid highway program last authorized under P.L. 109-59 (SAFETEA-LU). The Senate committee report (S.Rept. 111-69) to the FY2010 DOT Appropriations Act (P.L. 111-117) designates $7 million for the Marine Highway Initiative (the Administration had requested $15 million).

CAN MARINE HIGHWAYS DELIVER TANGIBLE BENEFITS?

A prevailing perception is that the slow speed of barges and the additional cargo transfer costs at ports deter use of marine highways. The fact that few containers are transported on such expansive internal U.S. waterway systems as the Mississippi River (including the Illinois, Ohio, and Missouri Rivers) and the Great Lakes suggests that there are deterrents.[5] However, there are also highly specific conditions under which barges might be an attractive option for container shippers. A brief survey of existing and defunct domestic waterborne container services points to specific circumstances in which this could occur. Three market segments can be identified and described as (1) short-distance ferries, (2) upriver inland container-on-barge (COB), and (3) coastal feeder services.

Short-Distance Ferries

Sometimes the shortest distance between two points happens to be over water. A ferry can be a particularly attractive alternative for freight if the overland route requires travel through a heavily congested area. The ferry across Lake Michigan between Ludington, MI, and Manitowoc, WI, which avoids the longer route around the south end of the lake through Chicago, is one example. Another is a ferry across Long Island Sound that allows trucks to travel between Long Island and New England without taking the longer route over bridges in New York City. These ferries carry both cars and trucks. Tellingly, a ferry service between Rochester, NY, and Toronto, Canada, over Lake Ontario did not stay in business for long, in part because it did not save truckers much time compared to the highway route.

The advantage of a truck ferry service is that the transition from land to water and back to land is seamless: the truck drives onto the ferry and then off again, with no separate cargo handling required. Truck ferries demonstrate that marine highways can be successful. However, the geography of the contiguous United States presents few opportunities for cross-waterway ferries.

Upriver Inland Port

Another potential market for marine highways can be identified as upriver inland feeder ports. Several coastal hub ports have satellite ports located upriver that could serve as potential inland container staging areas. Examples are Albany, NY; Richmond, VA; Memphis, TN; Sacramento and Stockton, CA; and Lewiston, ID.[6]

All of these river routes have railroads that parallel them. While river barges carry substantial amounts of lower-value cargoes in bulk and typically offer a lower rate than the railroads, the marine highway concept is predicated on diverting containerized cargo, typically the higher-value cargoes. Shippers of high-value goods are typically willing to pay more for faster transport. Railroads carry about 12 million truck trailers and containers annually, roughly equivalent to the number of containers imported by sea and equivalent to the number of trucks that cross into the United States from Canada and Mexico. Intermodal rail becomes more competitive as shipment distance increases (starting at distances of at least 500 to 750 miles), because as distance increases, the cost differential between truck and rail widens while the transit time differential narrows. COB services may be more competitive with trucks for shipment distances under 500 miles or so.

The experiences of two defunct upriver inland port services and those of a successful service are helpful in assessing whether this type of marine highway can be successful. The Port Authority of New York and New Jersey began to look for other means of moving containerized cargo to and from its hinterland in order to bypass road, bridge, and tunnel congestion in and around New York City. In April 2003, in cooperation with the port, Columbia Coastal Transport began offering the Albany Express Barge service, a COB service up the Hudson River to the Port of Albany. The service received $5.3 million in federal CMAQ funding, as well as state and local funding, which allowed the barge to undercut the trucking rate by 10%. Upriver to Albany, the barge carried containers loaded mainly with bulk commodities such as logs and silicon, while on the downriver trip it carried primarily empty containers. In addition to the longer transit time (12 to 18 hours by barge versus three hours by truck), the barge sailed only once per week. By the time it ceased operating in February 2006, the barge service had transported a total of 8,486 containers (loaded and empty), or fewer than 30 containers per voyage.[7]

In contrast to the Albany service, the Columbia-Snake River System (465 miles) has a long-established COB service, operating since 1975. Along this river system, containers are loaded with forest products at Lewiston, ID; hay cubes at Pasco, WA; and refrigerated potato and meat products at Boardman, OR. The containers are transferred to oceangoing ships at a marine terminal in Portland, OR, and exported to Asia. The trans-Pacific container carriers offer the barge service as part of a through route, meaning that their customers do not have to make separate arrangements for the barge leg. Three barge operators compete for this cargo and in combination provide frequent service. Barge travel time from Lewiston, ID, to Portland is about 51 hours, versus truck travel time of about eight hours, but the cost of barge transport is roughly 25% less. The container-on-barge services are profitable because the barges carrying containers are included in tows alongside barges carrying petroleum, grain, and other bulk cargoes; container barges would not be profitable as a stand-alone service.[8]

Based somewhat on a similar business model, COB service operated between Memphis and New Orleans on the Mississippi River from 2004 to 2009. Baled cotton (a highly seasonal product) as well as lumber and glucose were loaded in containers and shipped to New Orleans for export on containerships. Barge transit took five days, compared to truck transit of six hours. The service has been discontinued, apparently for lack of northbound cargo.[9] The same carrier tried to establish COB service between Memphis and Louisville, but this also failed.

Characteristics of a Sustainable Container-on-Barge Service

The experiences of the Albany, Columbia-Snake, and Memphis COB operations point to important considerations in judging the viability of marine highways on inland waterways. One is that COB services cater to shippers of lower value, intermediate, or unfinished goods. This is made possible by the significant U.S. containerized trade imbalance. Historically, containerized imports have exceeded exports by a wide margin, especially in the trans-Pacific trade. Exporters can take advantage of otherwise empty containers that are being repositioned to Asia and Europe. Grain exporters, for example, traditionally loaded their commodities in bulk into railcars or barges at inland points and transferred them in bulk to oceangoing vessels at ports, but 6% of U.S. grain exports to Asia moved in containers in 2009.[10] This bolstered demand for COB services. Without the trade imbalance, U.S. exporters of lower-value goods would probably find it too expensive to ship by container, and they would not require container-on-barge services for the inland portion of their export shipments.

Shippers of lower-value goods generally are willing to trade off faster transit times for significantly lower rates (20% to 30% lower is suggested by one study).[11] They also tend to ship heavier cargoes for which over-the-road weight limits (restricting the weight of cargo inside a container or trailer to 44,000 lbs.) keep them from loading containers to their physical capacity (over 60,000 lbs).[12] Container shipment becomes more viable if a shipper is located on the water, not requiring a truck trip to the river terminal. In addition to the cargo transfer costs, each carrier has overhead (fixed) costs that it must recover from each shipment regardless of its distance. Therefore, a shipment involving multiple carriers (for instance, a trucker on one or both ends of a barge movement) will carry more overhead costs than a single-carrier shipment.

COB services may also be more successful if they follow the railroads' example and sell their service to truckers, ocean carriers, or freight arrangers (middlemen) rather than directly to shippers.[13] Many shippers of containerized cargo are used to contracting with just one carrier, which is responsible for door-to-door service even if the transport involves multiple modes. These shippers could be reluctant to arrange for individual legs of a shipment themselves.

Access to backhaul traffic is also important to economic viability, as the Albany and Memphis examples show. The Memphis service may not have been able to capture northbound import loads from New Orleans because import containers tend to be loaded with higher-value manufactured goods whose shippers attach a high value to time; these shippers would rather pay more for rapid truck or rail transportation than pay less for slow and infrequent barge transportation. Also, the New Orleans-Memphis container route faces stiff competition from the Houston-Memphis route. Houston is a preferred container port to New Orleans due to its proximity to the ocean and its more frequent containership service, and containers destined for Memphis can be transshipped by rail or truck from Houston with little or no loss of time. In the case of the Albany COB service, there may have been little available southbound container traffic to New York because the region is not a large producer of agricultural or natural resource commodities for which barge service might be competitive.

As is the case with intermodal rail, shipment density is important to the viability of marine highways. Sufficient volume is necessary so that the water carrier can provide enough service frequency to compete with trucking's scheduling flexibility. If container barges can be incorporated into tows of bulk commodities, customers can be offered more frequent service, which may lead to greater demand.

Prospects for Federally Funded COB Services

The lessons learned from the above services shed light on the prospects for the COB services that have received grant funding. As indicated in *Table 1*, the James River 64 Express barge hopes to expand its service. At the Port of Richmond, VA, container volume has plummeted because the port recently lost the one regularly scheduled transatlantic container line that provided direct service.[14] However, former customers of this line that still require Richmond service may use the James River 64 Express Barge service as a replacement. Unlike the Albany barge service, this may provide the Richmond barge service with a relatively diverse base of customers. Companies producing tobacco products, paper, and quarry stone, all headquartered in Richmond, have expressed interest in the service. The service is predicated on highway, tunnel, and bridge congestion in the Norfolk area. As of August 2010, the James River barge was carrying 100 to 200 containers per week, and has been able to carry loaded containers in both directions. The river transit takes 12 hours while the truck transit takes two hours.[15]

The $30 million in federal funding for the Ports of Stockton and West Sacramento is to promote barge connections with the Port of Oakland. There is no current container service at these upriver ports to build upon. The business plan for the proposed services involves the transfer of cargo between international marine containers and larger domestic containers in Stockton and West Sacramento. The contents of three 40-foot international marine containers can be loaded into just two 53-foot domestic containers.[16] Consequently, some importers and exporters find it economical to pay the additional cost of transferring the cargo between equipment sizes at a warehouse (referred to as "cross docking") in the vicinity of the coastal port so that they can pay for the cost of moving just two rather than three containers overland. For these shippers, the inland transport leg is broken up into two segments: trucking the international container between the seaport and the warehouse where the cross docking occurs, and moving the domestic container between this warehouse and the final U.S. destination/origin. Thus, additional cargo handling operations, often the deterrent to COB service, are essentially negated because these shippers are already choosing an additional transloading step in order to utilize larger domestic containers.

A distinguishing feature of the Port of Oakland is that it is an important gateway for containerized exports to Asia. For this reason, it tends to have a relatively balanced flow of import and export containers. However, many of the container cargoes exported through Oakland are temperature controlled agricultural products such as meat. These are time-sensitive, high-value goods that typically move overland by truck because of their high service demands; intermodal rail has not been able to capture much of this cargo even for long-distance shipments. Although, as indicated above, an exporter of refrigerated products uses Columbia-Snake COB services, perishables are not generally considered good candidates for the proposed California barge services.

The Tenn-Tom COB project is also a new service. The service originates at the Port of Mobile, where a new container terminal opened in December 2008. The other terminus is the Port of Itawamba in northeast Mississippi. One expected customer is the furniture industry near the Port of Itawamba. These companies' imports from Asia currently move through the West Coast to

Memphis via intermodal rail and then to the factories by truck. Another potential user is Weyerhaeuser, which has two plants in the region and exports to Europe and Asia by truck through the ports of Charleston and Savannah. One hurdle for the new service is that the ports these two potential customers currently use offer much more frequent sailings to Asia and Europe than Mobile does.

As indicated in *Table 1*, the new ports being constructed on the Mississippi River at Granite City, IL, and Cates Landing, TN, are not solely targeting shippers of containerized cargo. These new ports are hoping to attract any cargo, including shippers of bulk commodities. The literature on these projects does not specifically describe potential container shipping customers nor the origins and destinations of cargo traveling through the ports.

Coastal Feeder Service

A third type of marine highway runs between ports along the coast. The cross-Gulf COB service between Brownsville, TX, and Port Manatee, FL, is the only coastal service that received federal funding. The water route between these two ports is about 600 miles shorter than the land route. In 2009, its first year of service, it carried the equivalent of 3,000 containers, or roughly 60 containers per week. The service caters to overweight cargo from Monterrey, Mexico, and, according to the carrier, provides savings of up to $1,000 per container shipment compared with the trucking alternative.[17] It has also been able to find some backhaul cargo.

Another Gulf of Mexico coastal operator, Osprey Lines, used to provide weekly service between Houston and Tampa with a stop at New Orleans on the return trip. It converted an offshore supply vessel, the *Sea Trader*, for container carriage. The *Sea Trader* capitalized on poor rail service between Texas and Florida and the reluctance of truckers to serve this market. However, scheduled coastwise service proved unviable because of a lack of westbound cargo. Ports located on the peninsular part of Florida, like Tampa, primarily serve local markets, and finding backhaul cargo to New Orleans and Houston proved difficult. Osprey Lines currently serves only the Houston-New Orleans route, and only when cargo is available rather than on a regularly scheduled basis.

Along the West Coast, Matson Navigation provided weekly container shuttle service between Los Angeles, Oakland, and Vancouver, Canada, from mid-1994 to the end of 2000. Unlike most marine highway services in recent years, Matson used a containership in this service. However, when a containership in its Hawaii service had to be replaced, Matson chose the shuttle vessel as the replacement. The shuttle service was only marginally profitable, and rather than acquire another vessel for the service, Matson contracted with a railroad to shuttle the containers.

Columbia Coastal Transport, the company that operated the COB service between the Port of New York and New Jersey and Albany, currently offers twice-weekly service between Norfolk and Baltimore. Its experience suggests that there may be a market for marine highways between hub ports and nearby ports that trans-oceanic containerships prefer to skip. Containership owners prefer to keep their expensive vessels moving by minimizing the number of port calls and avoiding ports that involve lengthy bay or river transits, like Baltimore. Columbia Coastal's barges provide feeder service to Baltimore for international containerships calling at Norfolk. The service carries almost 2,000 containers per week.[18] It formerly offered a similar feeder service between Boston and New York, but abandoned it in August 2010 because more international container vessels began calling at Boston directly.

The enlarged Panama Canal will accommodate larger containerships from 2015. There may be more opportunities for feeder services along the Atlantic and Gulf coasts if more large containerships from Asia call directly at East and Gulf Coast hub ports rather than unloading their cargo at Pacific Coast ports.

Growth Prospects for Marine Highway Services

Marine highway services, with the exception of those across the Great Lakes, cater primarily to the domestic portion of international containerized freight shipments. Domestic shipments are much less likely to use marine highways because, even with highway congestion, shippers are accustomed to relatively consistent on-time performance. Importers and exporters of containerized freight, on the other hand, are accustomed to delays routinely caused by weather, customs, and labor unrest here or overseas. In the context of an ocean voyage lasting two or three weeks, a one- or two-day delay is not unexpected or calamitous.[19]

In addition, a significant portion of domestic truck freight is carried in truck trailers rather than in containers that can be detached from their chassis. Barge services can carry truck trailers, but doing so is relatively inefficient, as trailers, unlike containers, cannot be stacked.

These factors severely limit the potential universe of truck traffic that marine highways could divert from the highways. International shipments account for less than one-tenth of total truck tonnage. The vast majority of the trucks contributing to highway congestion are serving routes or carrying products for which short-sea transport is not a viable alternative, or else are not designed to haul detachable ocean shipping containers.

VESSEL AND PORT TECHNOLOGY

Technological developments have been instrumental in helping railroads compete to carry truck trailers and containers.[20] Proponents of marine highways have suggested that similar developments might occur in the maritime sector, with changes in port or vessel technologies potentially driving down the cost of short-sea shipping. Funding technological development could be an option for promoting marine highways.

One such technology is "fast ferries," ships with speeds of 40 knots or greater, which have been proposed as a way to make coastal shipping more attractive. However, the fuel costs of these vessels could be prohibitive. For shippers, transit time on short-sea routes is much more a function of service frequency than of vessel speed: the need to wait one or two days for a scheduled vessel departure more than cancels out any gain from a faster vessel.

Another technological approach would be renewed emphasis on roll-on/roll-off (Ro/Ro) vessels, which have ramps to allow trucks to drive on and off, leaving just the trailer on the vessel. Ro/Ro vessels first came into wide use during World War II, and at various times have been used for coastal shipping. The advantage of Ro/Ros is that they do not require expensive gantry cranes to load and unload containers and can be loaded or unloaded quickly.[21] However, because the containers or truck trailers carried on the ships have wheels attached, they cannot be stacked on the ship or in the port, making the Ro/Ro concept much less space efficient.

Regardless of ship type, the Matson experience on the West Coast suggests that the capital costs of a dedicated ship can be a difficult hurdle, even in the U.S. coastal container market with the largest volume. Perhaps for this reason, U.S. coastal shipping services typically use oceangoing barges, with a tug either pulling or pushing the barge tow, rather than self-propelled containerships.[22] Crew size requirements are based on the tonnage of a vessel, which in the case of tug and barges is the tonnage of the tug, not the barge. For this reason, tug-and-barge combinations offer substantial savings in crewing costs, requiring crews of six to eight instead of 20 to 23 for self-propelled vessels.[23]

The lesson of avoiding high capital costs seems also to be relevant to cargo-handling equipment in ports. Rather than more expensive gantry cranes, reach stackers appear to be the prevalent means of loading and unloading container barges. A reach stacker is similar to a large fork lift but is mounted with a crane instead of a lift. Reducing cargo handling costs at ports is key to marine highway development.

ISSUES FOR CONGRESS

The main issue for Congress with respect to short-sea shipping is whether federal investment in marine highways will produce public benefits that outweigh the costs.

As the above analysis suggests, marine highways may be commercially viable in certain circumstances. In many instances, however, they have succeeded in capturing only a negligible share of container shipments along a given route.

There are questions, therefore, whether marine highways will divert enough trucks to provide public benefits commensurate with their costs.[24] For instance, at the height of its service, the Albany Express Barge was diverting 10 trucks a day. To put this number in perspective, the Port of New York and New Jersey handles, on average, about 10,000 containers per day.

Most of the marine highway services that have received federal grants are carrying, or seem likely to carry, no more than a few thousand containers annually.

On a per truck basis, therefore, the federal cost of diversion is likely to be in the neighborhood of several hundred dollars. Using the example of Albany Express Barge again, the $5.3 million of federal funding provided for this service enabled the transportation of 8,486 containers over the service's three-year life.

This equates to a federal outlay of $625 per container, which is in the neighborhood of what a shipper would pay for trucking a container between New York and Albany. Thus, the federally supported project roughly doubled the nation's freight bill for these container movements.

The Harbor Maintenance Tax

Another means of promoting short-sea shipping would be to repeal the existing harbor maintenance tax as it pertains to containerized domestic shipments, although the tax remains largely unenforced with respect to domestic shippers. The harbor maintenance tax, enacted in 1986, is essentially a federal port use charge intended to recover some of the costs incurred by the U.S. Army Corps of Engineers to operate and maintain waterside infrastructure in coastal and Great Lakes ports. These costs consist mostly of dredging navigation channels, but also maintaining breakwaters and jetties and operating several locks. (The harbor maintenance tax does not recover the Corps of Engineers' costs associated with the infrastructure of the inland waterway system, which is funded from a separate barge fuel tax.[25])

The harbor maintenance tax is assessed at 0.125% of shipment value ($1.25 per $1,000 of shipment value) on imported waterborne and domestic cargo. It is not assessed on waterborne exports, as a 1998 Supreme Court decision found this tax on exports to be unconstitutional. In addition to the amount of the tax, some have claimed that the administrative burden of payment on the part of the shipper discourages would-be waterborne shippers. While highway users also pay federal user charges (taxes on diesel fuel, new truck equipment, and truck weight charges), shippers do not pay these taxes directly; motor carriers do.

Waterborne importers pay the harbor maintenance tax as part of the Customs clearance process upon arrival of the shipment, while domestic shippers pay the tax on a quarterly basis. Domestic shippers are charged only once for each shipment, not at both ports. However, if imported goods are offloaded from a vessel at one port and then shipped to another U.S. port on a different vessel, such as a feeder ship or barge, the tax would be assessed at both ports. The tax thus discourages domestic water shipment of import and export containers.

The tax could also be particularly cumbersome for domestic vessel operators carrying containers of mixed cargo assembled by consolidators, because these typically hold shipments from multiple customers. Before using a marine highway, the vessel operator would need to assure that each shipper was advised that it would be subject to the tax.

In the 111th Congress, bills were introduced that would have exempted containerized domestic shipments from paying the harbor maintenance tax.[26] However, according to preliminary estimates by the Corps of Engineers, only about 10% of what is potentially owed is being collected from domestic shippers.[27] The Corps also estimates that waterborne shippers pay about 10% of the federal cost of providing navigation infrastructure, either through the harbor maintenance tax or the barge fuel tax.[28] This compares with highway user fees (including truck-specific taxes and fees) that cover most of the federal cost of highway infrastructure and railroads, which by and large privately finance their infrastructure. Thus, legislation that further reduces the financial burden on waterway users raises equity and economic efficiency issues with respect to competing modes.

The Jones Act

A long-standing U.S. law commonly referred to as the Jones Act (46 U.S.C. § 55102) requires that only American-built, -owned, and -crewed vessels can operate between two U.S. ports.[29] The law dates back to 1920 and was enacted on the grounds that a domestic maritime industry is necessary for national and economic security.

If not for the Jones Act, domestic containers could be shipped between U.S. coastal ports on existing services provided by international carriers. Foreign containerships carrying U.S. imports and exports already sail frequently between U.S. ports, providing an almost continuous conveyor belt of vessel space along each coast. These ships typically call at three or four ports along a coastal region, and since they generally unload a good portion of the ship's cargo at the first port call, they would have empty space to carry domestic containers to the other U.S. ports on their schedule. However, because they are not in compliance with the Jones Act, these vessels are not allowed to pick up shipments in one U.S. port and unload them at another.

Since the construction cost of U.S.-flag deepwater cargo ships is generally believed to be three or four times that of ships in the world market, the Jones Act may be a significant barrier to domestic shipping in oceangoing vessels.30 As of year-end 2008 (latest data available), there were 42 active Jones Act-compliant ships suitable for deepwater marine highway service, including 27 containerships and 15 Ro-Ro ships.31 Of these, 29 (70%) were built before 1984 and thus approaching the end of their useful lives, normally 20 to 25 years for saltwater vessels. The United States is the only industrialized nation that has a domestic build requirement for domestic shipping, and no such requirement exists for other U.S. freight modes. The use of barges in marine highway services is also subject to Jones Act requirements, but the additional

End Notes

[1] 75 FR 18095, April 9, 2010.

[2] See section 55605 of P.L. 110-140.

[3] 75 FR 49017, August 12, 2010.

[4] TIGER I was authorized in the American Recovery and Reinvestment Act (P.L. 111-5) under Title XII, providing $1.5 billion in DOT discretionary grants for DOT; TIGER II was authorized in the FY2010 DOT Appropriations Act (P.L. 111-117). CMAQ is a federal-aid highway program last authorized under P.L. 109-59 (SAFETEA-LU). The Senate Committee Report (S.Rept. 111-69) to the FY2010 DOT Appropriations Act (P.L. 111-117) designates $7 million for the Marine Highway Initiative (the Administration had requested $15 million).

[5] The Port of Montreal is the fourth-largest container port on the North American East Coast. Despite the fact that half of the containers passing through the port have a U.S. origin or destination, none of them travel over the Great Lakes.

[6] Augusta, GA, geographically fits this description as well but there have not been any feeder services on this river for some time nor does there appear to be any discussion of them for the future.

[7] New York State DOT letter to MARAD regarding the Marine Highway Initiative, dated February 6, 2009. Available at http://www.regulations.gov under docket # MARAD-2008-0096.

[8] Transportation Research Board, National Cooperative Freight Research Program, Report 5, North American Marine Highways, 2010, p. 33.

[9] Transportation Research Board, National Cooperative Freight Research Program, Report 5, North American Marine Highways, 2010, p. 62.

[10] U.S. Department of Agriculture, Agricultural Marketing Service, Grain Transportation Report, December 30, 2010, p. 20, http://www.ams.usda.gov/AMSv1.0/ getfile?dDocName= STELPRDC5088382.

[11] Transportation Research Board, National Cooperative Freight Research Program, Report 5, North American Marine Highways, 2010, p. 3.

[12] For cargoes with high weight-to-volume ratios, container shippers can use a 20-foot container rather than a 40-foot container, but the rate is reduced by something less than 50%. Over-the-road weight limits are higher in Canada, Mexico, and generally overseas.

[13] Intermodal marketing companies, similar to freight forwarders, make the door-to-door arrangements for intermodal rail shipments.

[14] The draft of the James River is 25 feet, so this shipping line used smaller vessels than are typical for trans-ocean containerships. The shipping line is now calling at Wilmington, NC, instead of Richmond, VA.

[15] The issue of whether there is enough freight to sustain both rail and barge container services is especially applicable to the federal funding provided to this marine highway project because federal funding has also been provided to streamline the rail connection and rail corridor leading to the Port of Norfolk.

[16] An "international" container can be shipped domestically, but a "domestic" container is not designed for maritime use. A domestic container is slightly wider than a standard container. A 40-foot international marine container has an internal capacity of 2,390 cubic feet versus 3,850 cubic feet for a 53-foot domestic container or trailer.

[17] Transport Topics, SeaBridge Freight to Launch U.S. – Mexico Barge Service, November 17, 2008.

[18] 73 FR 59531.

[19] U.S. railroads have also found it much easier to meet the needs of international container shippers than of domestic container shippers. The intermodal freight they haul is overwhelmingly part of an import or export shipment.

[20] These developments include the "well-car" that allows for double stacking of containers, articulated cars that reduce cargo damage, and innovations like the "roadrailer" (trailers with both rubber and steel wheels) that has been marketable in specific corridors.

[21] Transportation Research Board, National Cooperative Freight Research Program, Report 5, North American Marine Highways, 2010, p. 16.

[22] Ocean barges as well as self-propelled ships are used for shipments between the mainland and Alaska and Puerto Rico, but ocean barges are not used in service to Hawaii; that is, ocean barges are limited to coastal rather than transoceanic voyages.

[23] Transportation Research Board, National Cooperative Freight Research Program, Report 5, North American Marine Highways, 2010, p. 15.

[24] Moreover, trucks account for only 8% of highway vehicle miles traveled. For further analysis on congestion and potential solutions, see CRS Report RL33995, Surface Transportation Congestion: Policy and Issues.

[25] For further information on the legislative history and implementation of the tax, see CRS Report R41042, Harbor Maintenance Trust Fund Expenditures.

[26] See H.R. 638, H.R. 3486, S. 551, S. 1509.

[27] FY2011 USACE Budget Justification, p. RIO – 66. As a result of a GAO audit, USACE and Customs (CBP) are sharing shipping information in order to improve enforcement of the tax.

[28] John Paul Woodley, Jr., then Assistant Secretary of the Army for Civil Works, press conference announcing the FY2008 USACE Civil Works Budget, February 5, 2007.

[29] The law also requires that they be U.S. owned and crewed. 46 U.S.C. 55102.

[30] The Jones Act applies to Alaska, Hawaii, and Puerto Rico (with an exception for passengers), while other U.S. possessions and territories are partially or fully exempted. The Jones Act carriers serving these markets are under a Department of Justice (DOJ) investigation for price-fixing; several executives from two of the carriers have pleaded guilty with respect to the Puerto Rico trade. Civil antitrust lawsuits are also proceeding.

[31] MARAD, U.S. Water Transportation Statistical Snapshot (12/7/09 updated version), p. 18. Dry bulk lakers (47) and oil tankers (51) account for two-thirds of the Jones Act fleet.

In: America's Marine Highways
Editor: Rafael Pelletier

ISBN: 978-1-62618-857-0
© 2013 Nova Science Publishers, Inc.

Chapter 3

AMERICA'S MARINE HIGHWAY FREQUENTLY ASKED QUESTIONS[*]

U.S. Department of Transportation, Maritime Administration

WHAT ARE AMERICA'S MARINE HIGHWAYS?

America's Marine Highways are navigable waterways that have been designated by the Secretary of Transportation and have demonstrated the ability to provide additional capacity to relieve congested landside routes serving freight and passenger movement.

Each marine highway has a corridor designation that reflects the congested landside route it parallels.

For example, M-95 stretches from Maine to Florida and is the designation for the shipping lane along the Atlantic Coast paralleling interstate highway I-95.

---

[*] This is an edited, reformatted and augmented version of U.S. Department of Transportation, Maritime Administration.

Who Should I Contact in My Region to Talk about America's Marine Highway Program?

Please contact your local Maritime Administration (MARAD) Gateway Office (http://www.marad.dot.gov/documents/OFFICE_OF_ GATEWAYS_Telephone_Listing.pdf) for more information.

What Is the Difference between Marine Highways and Short Sea Shipping?

Short sea shipping commonly refers to coast-wise waterborne transportation of freight and or passengers by navigable waterways without crossing an ocean.

Marine Highways are short sea routes and inland water routes within the US that have been designated by the Secretary of Transportation. America's Marine Highway Program, administered by the Maritime Administration, was formed to help develop new and expand existing U.S. flag services that transport passengers and/or containerized or trailerized freight along Marine Highways.

What's the Difference between a Corridor, Connector and Crossing?

Corridors, Connectors, and Crossings identify routes where water transportation presents an opportunity to offer relief to landside corridors that suffer from traffic congestion, excessive air emissions or other environmental concerns and other challenges.

Corridors are generally longer, multi-state routes whereas Connectors represent shorter routes that serve as feeders to the larger Corridors. Crossings are short routes that transit harbors or waterways and offer alternatives to much longer or less convenient land routes between points.

How Do I Apply for Designation as a Corridor, Connector or Crossing?

Corridor, connector, and crossing applications from public entities are always welcome. Contents of the application include a narrative portion that should not exceed 20 pages in length. Applications may be submitted electronically via the Marine Highway e-mail address (mh@dot.gov). Please mail a hard copy to the Administrator of the Maritime Administration, Mr. David T. Matsuda 1200 New Jersey Ave., SE Washington, DC 20590-0001 Room W22-318, MAR-100. Instructions regarding applications are included in the Final Rule (http://www.marad.dot.gov/ships_shipping_landing_page/mhi_home/mhi_domestic_shipping/MHP_Hot_Topics_(In_the_News).htm#) for America's Marine Highway program published April 9, 2010. For more info, contact a Gateway Office Director (http://www.marad.dot.gov/documents/OFFICE_OF_GATEWAYS_Telephone_Listing.pdf) in your region.

What Is the Difference between a Designated Project and a Designated Initiative?

Designated projects have been recognized by the Secretary of Transportation as having the ability to create new marine highway services or expand existing services. Project designations are obtained through an application process. The first "Call for Projects" applications were held in 2010. Calls for projects are published by the Federal Register approximately every 2 years. Designated initiatives are recognized by the Secretary as being potential projects that have not yet been developed to the point of proposing specific services and routes required of project designation. For more information, contact your local Maritime Administration Gateway Office.

What Are the Benefits of Being Designated a Marine Highway Project?

Designated projects receive preferential treatment from the Department and MARAD. In addition to possible funding assistance, the Office of Marine Highways supported by the Gateway Offices may provide other support services (http://www.marad.dot.gov/documents/Final_Rule_Excerpt_MH_Project_Criteria_April_2010.pdf). Once project designation has been received, you do not need to apply in future calls for projects. However, a letter updating the status of your project is required to be submitted every two (2) years. Project designation will remain with the public sponsor of the project unless the project has substantially changed.

I HAVE BEEN DESIGNATED AN INITIATIVE; MAY I APPLY FOR PROJECT DESIGNATION IN THE FUTURE?

Absolutely! You would be eligible during the next "Call for Projects" and a complete updated application meeting all criteria would be required for consideration. Contact your local Gateway Office (http://www.marad.dot.gov/documents/OFFICE_OF_GATEWAYS_Telephone_Listing.pdf) for more information.

Original link to these FAQs (visited March 2013): http://www.marad.dot.gov/ships_shipping_landing_page/mhi_home/mhi_domestic_shipping/MHP_Hot_Topics_%28In_the_News%29.htm

INDEX

A

access, 10, 13, 14, 16, 17, 19, 24, 33, 46, 57, 76, 97
accounting, 22
actuality, 54
ad valorem tax, 71
adaptations, 61
advancements, 11
adverse effects, 37
Afghanistan, 33
age, 31
agencies, ix, 4, 7, 31, 32, 44, 46, 47, 48, 50, 69, 74, 78, 80, 81, 90
air emissions, 31, 44, 118
air pollutants, 29, 93
air quality, 11, 30, 45, 52, 55, 56, 69, 93
Alaska, 57, 116
alternative energy, 57
American Recovery and Reinvestment Act, ix, 2, 4, 11, 43, 54, 75, 92, 94, 97, 103, 115
American Recovery and Reinvestment Act of 2009, ix, 2, 4, 11, 43, 54, 75, 92, 94, 97
ammonia, 38, 91, 92
antitrust, 116
appropriate technology, 24
appropriations, x, 5, 79

Appropriations Act, 11, 43, 103, 115
aquatic habitats, 31
arguably, xi, 53, 100
Asia, 105, 106, 108, 110
assessment, 86, 92, 96
assets, x, 6, 40, 66, 71
atmosphere, 27
audit, 116
authorities, 42, 55, 68, 74, 75, 80, 93, 101
authority, ix, 4, 42, 70
automobiles, 18, 25, 37
awareness, 52, 69

B

barriers, 49, 77, 79
base, 16, 33, 36, 62, 102, 107
benchmarks, 52
beneficiaries, 73, 75, 76
benefits, vii, viii, x, xi, 3, 5, 8, 9, 10, 11, 22, 23, 27, 29, 30, 31, 32, 42, 44, 45, 46, 49, 50, 52, 54, 55, 56, 57, 62, 63, 67, 68, 70, 71, 73, 77, 78, 79, 80, 82, 85, 89, 92, 100, 101, 112
Boat, 69
border crossing, 19, 53
BTU, 1, 24, 26, 89
bulk materials, 13
Bureau of Labor Statistics, 15, 37, 87, 90

122 Index

burn, 29, 61
business model, ix, 5, 54, 57, 95, 106
business strategy, 57
businesses, 17, 20, 38
butadiene, 91

C

candidates, 44, 108
carbon, 29, 51, 55, 89
carbon dioxide, 29
carbon emissions, 29, 51
carbon monoxide, 55
cargoes, ix, xi, 5, 19, 22, 23, 26, 27, 32, 33, 37, 39, 40, 46, 47, 54, 57, 60, 61, 63, 77, 79, 92, 100, 104, 106, 108, 115
cash, 74
cash flow, 74
catalyst, 51
CBP, 1, 72, 96, 116
certificate, 16
CFR, 87, 90
challenges, 19, 44, 54, 57, 77, 78, 82, 95, 118
chemical, 39
chemicals, 92
Chicago, 14, 19, 88, 104
children, 90
China, 27
chlorine, 38, 91, 92
cities, 15, 39, 57, 68
citizens, 33, 64
City, 92, 102, 104, 105, 109
classes, 85
Clean Air Act, 30
cleanup, 39
climate, 11
closure, 41
CO2, 1, 29, 70
coal, x, 26, 99, 100
Coast Guard, 3, 15
coastal region, 114
collaboration, 51

combined effect, 30
combustion, 29
commensurate, xi, 100, 112
commerce, vii, 6, 21
commercial, 8, 9, 24, 28, 33, 34, 36, 37, 50, 54, 60, 80, 88
commodity, 26, 89
communities, 31
community, 62, 69, 70, 71, 78, 95
compatibility, 10
compensation, 94
competition, 107
competitiveness, 49, 65
compliance, 33, 44, 52, 114
computer, 9
conference, 96, 116
configuration, 50
Congress, v, vii, ix, xi, 1, 3, 4, 10, 11, 16, 42, 48, 72, 74, 75, 78, 80, 94, 96, 99, 100, 101, 112, 113
conservation, 51
Consolidated Appropriations Act, ix, 4, 11, 42, 75, 92, 93, 96, 97
consolidation, 57
construction, 16, 31, 34, 36, 45, 50, 56, 60, 61, 71, 73, 75, 97, 114
consumers, 68
consumption, 24, 25, 27
containers, viii, x, 3, 5, 8, 13, 14, 15, 16, 20, 22, 29, 41, 50, 54, 55, 56, 57, 61, 63, 66, 71, 72, 74, 79, 83, 84, 85, 100, 103, 105, 106, 107, 108, 109, 110, 111, 112, 113, 114, 115, 116
contingency, 32, 34, 38
conversations, 42
cooperation, 12, 47, 50, 78, 88, 92, 105
coordination, 31, 47, 62, 71, 78, 80, 82, 96
cost, viii, xi, 3, 8, 9, 10, 11, 17, 18, 20, 21, 22, 29, 32, 33, 34, 39, 40, 49, 50, 51, 55, 56, 57, 60, 62, 63, 64, 65, 71, 72, 77, 85, 89, 95, 100, 101, 105, 108, 111, 112, 114

Index

cost saving, 49, 50, 56, 57, 63, 72, 89
cotton, 106
covering, 101
creating, viii, 3, 64
credentials, 16
credit market, 76
culture, 13
curriculum, 16
customers, 57, 66, 68, 78, 96, 105, 107, 109, 113
Customs and Border Protection, 1, 72, 96

D

damages, 92
danger, 39
data collection, 47
DCA, 91
decision makers, 52, 54
Department of Commerce, 78
Department of Defense, 1, 33, 47, 90
Department of Energy, 3, 7, 24, 25, 26, 28, 85, 89
Department of Homeland Security, 92
Department of Justice, 116
Department of Transportation, v, viii, xi, 1, 3, 4, 18, 45, 56, 57, 85, 86, 87, 88, 89, 90, 91, 92, 93, 94, 95, 96, 97, 99, 101, 117
deposits, 50
depreciation, x, 5, 73, 79
deregulation, 84
description, ix, 5, 44, 84, 90, 115
dialogues, 47
diesel engines, 30, 51
diesel fuel, 26, 29, 30, 55, 57, 61, 89, 113
direct cost, 71
directional, xi, 100
disaster, 41
discharges, 31
displacement, 30
distribution, 55
DOJ, 116

domestic shippers, xi, 100, 113, 114
DOT, xi, 55, 93, 94, 97, 99, 101, 103, 115
draft, 14, 34, 115

E

earnings, 15
economic competitiveness, viii, 3, 7, 12
economic efficiency, 8, 114
economic growth, 21
education, 13
electricity, 7, 28
e-mail, 94, 119
emergency, 7, 15, 16, 33, 34, 37, 41, 92
emergency preparedness, 7
emergency relief, 33, 41
emergency response, 33
emission, 30
employment, 15, 17, 32, 37, 80, 87
employment opportunities, 15
encouragement, 78
endorsements, 87
energy, viii, 4, 7, 10, 11, 12, 24, 26, 27, 29, 31, 44, 45, 49, 51, 52, 55, 60, 67, 75, 89, 96
energy conservation, 12, 31, 52
energy consumption, 7, 10, 24, 26, 45, 89
energy efficiency, 51, 67, 75
Energy Independence and Security Act, vii, xi, 1, 3, 80, 86, 92, 99, 101
energy security, 51
enforcement, 22, 88, 116
engineering, 9
environment, 9, 32, 38, 49, 50, 60, 64, 73, 77
environmental effects, 31
environmental factors, 51
environmental impact, 12, 30, 31, 50, 61
environmental issues, 31
environmental protection, 61
Environmental Protection Agency, ix, 1, 4, 51, 82, 84, 90
environmental quality, 52

124 Index

environmental standards, 75, 76
environmental sustainability, 7, 8, 10, 12, 24, 78, 97
environments, 32
EPA, ix, 1, 4, 7, 25, 28, 30, 32, 43, 48, 49, 51, 52, 57, 67, 78, 80, 90, 93
equipment, ix, x, xi, 5, 10, 14, 18, 31, 34, 38, 41, 51, 57, 60, 61, 62, 63, 64, 71, 73, 75, 76, 79, 88, 91, 100, 108, 112, 113
equity, xi, 76, 100, 114
erosion, 31
EU, 1, 12, 13
Europe, viii, 3, 13, 14, 61, 63, 77, 86, 106, 109
European Commission, 67, 86, 95
European Regional Development Fund, 12
European Union, 1, 12
evacuation, 41
examinations, 16
exercise, 42
expand, vii, 3, 11, 20, 54, 57, 65, 73, 107, 118, 119
expenditures, 73
expertise, 48
exporter, 108
exporters, 20, 23, 56, 57, 106, 108, 110
exports, 7, 13, 106, 108, 109, 113, 114
exposure, 37
external benefits, 10
external costs, 63, 85, 86

F

factories, 109
faith, 76
families, 13
Federal funds, 49
federal government, 102
Federal Highway Administration, 1, 13, 18, 85, 86, 88, 89, 91
Federal Register, 46, 119

fencing, 60
FHWA, 1, 13, 19, 20, 22, 55, 88, 93, 97
financial, 61, 76, 114
financial support, 61
first responders, 40
fishing, 30, 91
flexibility, 17, 107
flooding, 102
food, 41
foreign ports, 72
foundations, 34
freight traffic, x, 5, 29, 78, 99
fuel consumption, 7, 25, 27, 34, 51, 55, 56, 67, 70, 73, 94
fuel efficiency, 25, 26, 28, 30, 52, 89
fuel prices, 11, 27
funding, ix, xi, 4, 12, 17, 46, 47, 48, 49, 54, 56, 57, 68, 70, 74, 77, 93, 95, 99, 101, 103, 105, 107, 108, 109, 112, 115, 119
funds, 11, 43, 46, 52, 54, 56, 74, 75, 93, 94, 95, 96, 102

G

GAO, 2, 19, 65, 85, 86, 88, 95, 96, 116
garbage, 91
geography, 7, 13, 101, 104
GHG, 2, 7, 9, 11, 25, 27, 28, 29, 30, 31, 51, 56, 89
glucose, 106
government assistance, ix, 5
government intervention, 62
government policy, viii, 3
grant funding, xi, 99, 107
grant programs, 75
grants, ix, x, 4, 5, 11, 43, 46, 47, 61, 69, 74, 75, 79, 93, 96, 97, 101, 103, 112, 115
greenhouse, viii, 3, 4, 24, 89
greenhouse gas, viii, 3, 4, 24, 89
greenhouse gas (GHG), viii, 4, 24
greenhouse gas emissions, viii, 3

Index

greenhouse gases, 89
Gross Domestic Product, 87
growth, 7, 11, 12, 13, 14, 15, 17, 21, 24, 28, 42, 64, 76, 96
guidelines, 50, 62
guilty, 116
Gulf Coast, 31, 41, 56, 57, 65, 102, 110
Gulf of Mexico, 109

H

habitats, 61
harbors, 44, 118
Hawaii, 57, 110, 116
hazardous materials, viii, 4, 8, 37, 38, 40, 57
health, 13, 30, 38, 90
health care, 13
height, 112
high fat, 9
high school, 16
Highlands, 87
highway congestion, x, 73, 99, 100, 110, 111
highway system, 22, 88
highways, xi, 9, 14, 19, 20, 21, 22, 23, 31, 37, 56, 57, 69, 88, 99, 100, 101, 103, 104, 106, 107, 110, 111, 112
history, vii, 6, 8, 13, 116
House, 84, 92, 96
House of Representatives, 84
House Report, 92, 96
hub, xi, 57, 100, 104, 110
human, 8, 16, 27, 38
human resources, 16
hurricanes, 27

I

ID, 104, 105
identification, 16, 44, 49
IMO, 2, 89

impairments, 23
imports, 7, 13, 20, 71, 106, 108, 114
improvements, 25, 30, 38, 49, 56, 60, 67, 76, 79, 82, 95
impurities, 30
income, 50, 74
income tax, 50
individuals, 15
industry, viii, ix, x, 4, 5, 7, 9, 12, 15, 16, 27, 30, 31, 32, 36, 38, 42, 48, 50, 51, 69, 71, 78, 79, 80, 94, 108, 114
inefficiency, 19, 61
INF, 89
infrastructure, ix, x, 5, 6, 7, 9, 10, 17, 19, 20, 22, 23, 32, 38, 39, 40, 41, 43, 45, 48, 57, 60, 61, 62, 63, 66, 67, 71, 73, 75, 76, 77, 79, 81, 85, 97, 101, 102, 103, 113, 114
initiation, ix, 4, 11
injury, 9, 91
integration, 66
integrity, 76
interface, 66
International Maritime Organization, 2, 29, 89
international trade, 21, 33
investment, x, 5, 9, 10, 21, 44, 55, 60, 61, 63, 73, 77, 78, 79, 85, 96, 112
investments, 9, 21, 61, 66, 67, 68, 70, 73, 75, 76, 80, 97
Iraq, 33
issues, xi, 12, 32, 38, 49, 60, 68, 77, 100, 114

J

jurisdiction, 68
justification, viii, 3

K

knots, 34, 111

L

lakes, 32, 87, 95
land-based, vii, x, 5, 6, 8, 13, 17, 19, 22, 25, 26, 29, 39, 57, 61, 62, 64, 66, 70, 72, 77, 79, 89
landfills, 31
landside congestion, viii, 3, 11, 44, 49, 81
laws, 52, 64, 88
laws and regulations, 52, 64
lead, 17, 25, 29, 30, 107
leadership, ix, x, 4, 6, 12, 31, 33, 42, 51, 78
legislation, ix, x, 4, 5, 11, 42, 48, 70, 80, 114
legs, 107
life cycle, 71
light, 8, 17, 24, 28, 107
light rail, 17
light trucks, 24, 28
liquefied natural gas, 92
livable communities, 49
loan guarantees, 76
loans, 61
local authorities, 68
local government, 11, 12, 46, 48, 80, 81, 82
logistics, 12, 33, 48, 72, 82, 84, 87, 96
lubricants, 52

M

majority, vii, 6, 15, 36, 60, 64, 111
management, 31, 57, 62, 77, 87
manmade disasters, viii, 4, 8, 37, 40
manufactured goods, 107
manufacturing, 33
marine highway, vii, xi, 31, 49, 99, 100, 101, 103, 104, 105, 106, 107, 109, 110, 111, 112, 113, 114, 115, 117, 119
Maritime Transportation Security Act, 16
market incentives, 70

market segment, 104
market share, 21
marketing, 57, 69, 115
materials, 9, 37, 38, 39, 40
matter, 2, 30, 33, 48
meat, 105, 108
memorandums of understanding, 82
metropolitan areas, vii, 6
Mexico, ix, 5, 53, 101, 105, 109, 115, 116
Miami, 87
Middle East, 33
military, 32, 33, 34, 36, 41
mission, 34
missions, viii, 4, 24, 33
Mississippi River, 102, 103, 106, 109
Missouri, 103
mitigate landside, vii, 3, 42, 80, 101
models, 54, 57
modifications, 60, 76
modules, 34
MR, 91
MTS, 2, 48, 49

N

National Ambient Air Quality Standards, 30
National Defense Authorization Act, ix, xi, 4, 11, 42, 92, 93, 96, 99, 101
national emergency, 10, 16, 32, 34
National Environmental Policy Act (NEPA), 32
national product, 17
national security, 9, 11, 16, 32, 33, 49, 80
national transportation system, 10, 19, 44, 77, 80
natural disaster, 8
New England, 57, 104
new freight, viii, 3, 10
next generation, 16
NHS, 2, 19
nitrogen, 30, 55
nodes, 14

Index

non-bulk freight, vii, x, 5, 6, 63
North America, ix, 5, 53, 90, 94, 95, 96, 115, 116
nucleus, 34

O

obstacles, xi, 71, 100
officials, 42, 53
OH, 87
oil, 17, 29, 41, 89, 100, 116
oil spill, 41
operating costs, 39, 61, 62, 63, 64
operations, ix, 5, 14, 16, 26, 29, 30, 31, 33, 34, 40, 41, 42, 50, 57, 60, 61, 63, 64, 65, 66, 68, 71, 78, 88, 91, 106, 108
opportunities, 7, 11, 17, 46, 51, 53, 66, 67, 69, 101, 104, 110
opportunity costs, 9
outreach, ix, 5, 34, 53, 77, 78
overhead costs, 106
overweight, 22, 23, 54, 56, 57, 88, 109
ownership, 66
ozone, 30

P

Pacific, 19, 105, 106, 110
paints, 52
Panama, 57, 110
parallel, vii, xi, 6, 49, 99, 100, 104
participants, 53, 82
Pasco, 105
peace, 10
petroleum, 7, 9, 25, 77, 84, 89, 105
Philadelphia, 87
pipeline, 84
plants, 109
playing, 64
PM, 2, 30
policy, 12, 39, 48, 52, 53, 67, 68, 70, 88
policymakers, 100

pollutants, 70
pollution, 24, 29, 30, 31, 63
population, vii, 6, 37, 57
potato, 105
potential benefits, 9, 13, 26, 54, 72
power generation, 25
power plants, 31
precedent, 12
preferential treatment, 46, 119
preponderance, vii, 6
present value, 49, 74
preservation, 68
President, 7, 25, 28, 93, 96, 97
primary, vii, 6, 39, 55, 63, 70, 73
private benefits, 69
private investment, 55
private sector, x, 6, 8, 12, 47, 48, 55, 66, 68, 71, 77, 81, 82, 85
private sector investment, 71
procurement, 36, 56, 73
producers, 17
profitability, 17, 67
project, 32, 33, 42, 45, 46, 49, 54, 55, 56, 75, 76, 79, 81, 82, 94, 96, 101, 108, 112, 115, 119, 120
prosperity, 9
protection, 97
public awareness, 60
public health, 9, 30
public investment, 21, 67
public resources, 10, 67
public safety, viii, 4, 7, 8, 10, 37, 56, 67, 89
public support, 29
public welfare, x, 5
Puerto Rico, 57, 116

Q

qualifications, 16, 90
quality of life, 13, 14, 17, 29, 32, 60
quality of service, 9
quality standards, 31

R

railroads, x, xi, 19, 29, 31, 39, 84, 89, 91, 92, 99, 100, 104, 107, 111, 114, 116
ramp, 62
reality, 54
recognition, 25, 27, 52, 67
recommendations, 43, 44, 49, 84
reconstruction, 50
recovery, 23, 37, 40, 41, 77
recreation, 13, 31
recreational, 30, 91
redundancy, 8, 15, 40, 41
regulations, 30, 32, 48, 64, 83, 115
regulatory framework, 32, 38
rehabilitation, 60
reimburse, 85
related research, ix, 4, 49
reliability, 9, 11, 17, 27, 65, 66, 67, 70
relief, 10, 14, 15, 44, 45, 55, 102, 118
reluctance, ix, 5, 65, 71, 109
repair, 10, 15, 33, 36, 77
requirements, viii, x, 4, 5, 11, 12, 15, 30, 34, 43, 48, 57, 61, 62, 64, 69, 76, 78, 79, 93, 96, 111, 114
researchers, 68
resiliency, viii, 3, 8, 23, 40, 49, 78
resources, viii, 4, 7, 8, 9, 11, 32, 38, 40, 61, 69, 77
response, 32, 37, 38, 39, 40, 41, 44, 68, 77, 92
restrictions, 57, 64, 88
retail, 57
revenue, 33, 70, 71
risk, 37, 38, 39, 71, 79
risks, 31, 32, 72
routes, vii, 6, 10, 14, 25, 27, 29, 37, 42, 44, 46, 50, 57, 66, 71, 79, 81, 88, 92, 101, 104, 111, 117, 118, 119
rubber, 116
rulemaking, viii, 4, 28
rules, 30, 43

S

sabotage, 39
safety, 7, 9, 11, 37, 38, 41, 44, 45, 49, 60, 62
saltwater, 114
savings, xi, 22, 23, 27, 34, 45, 49, 67, 71, 100, 109, 112
scale economies, 95
school, 16, 87
scope, 32, 73, 76
SEA, 80, 81, 83, 84
security, viii, 4, 8, 10, 37, 38, 45, 57, 60, 89, 92, 114
seed, 101
Senate, 84, 103, 115
September 11, 41, 92
service provider, 47, 48, 51, 54, 57, 61, 70, 71, 72, 73, 95, 96
shape, 26
shelter, 41
showing, 91
silicon, 105
skilled workers, 36
smog, 31
social costs, 84, 85
social responsibility, 51
societal cost, 39
society, 17
species, 31
specific tax, 114
spending, 17
stakeholder groups, 71
stakeholders, x, 5, 48, 55, 70, 73, 74, 76, 78
standardization, 34, 62, 71
state, 105, 118
states, 100, 101
statistics, 85, 86, 87, 91
statutes, 50
steel, 16, 41, 116
storage, 57, 61, 66
structure, 43, 44, 97

Index

129

sulfur, 30, 52, 55, 57
summarizes, viii, ix, 4, 70
suppliers, 17
supply chain, ix, 5, 17, 66
supply disruption, 25
support services, 66, 120
Supreme Court, 113
sustainability, 46, 61, 94, 101

T

tanks, 41
target, 10, 57
tax credits, x, 5, 73, 79, 96
tax policy, 70, 79
taxes, 74, 85, 113
teams, 41
technical assistance, 47, 74
techniques, 12, 63
technological developments, 8
technologies, 52, 66, 77, 84, 111
technology, 49, 82, 83, 84, 111
temperature, 108
terminals, 20, 50, 55, 60, 61, 63, 66, 75
terrorism, 40
terrorist attack, 41
three research studies, ix, 4, 46
time frame, xi, 99
Title I, 76, 97
tobacco, 107
total energy, 24
trade, 9, 36, 50, 70, 83, 84, 106, 116
training, 16, 40, 52, 87
transactions, 70
transit, xi, 11, 13, 14, 21, 44, 50, 57, 65,
    67, 68, 69, 92, 99, 100, 105, 106, 108,
    111, 118
transport, x, xi, 9, 12, 16, 21, 37, 38, 41,
    42, 47, 60, 61, 64, 67, 72, 82, 84, 86,
    95, 99, 100, 105, 107, 108, 111, 118
transportation infrastructure, 43, 49, 76,
    77

Transportation Security Administration,
    2, 16
transshipment, 14, 96
truck drivers, 17
Trust Fund, 71, 96, 116

U

U.S. Army Corps of Engineers, 32, 85,
    113
U.S. Bureau of Labor Statistics, 87
U.S. Department of Agriculture, 115
U.S. Department of Commerce, 90
U.S. Department of Labor, 87, 90
underutilized, x, 6, 20, 78
uniform, 64
unions, 16
unit cost, 57, 63
United, vii, x, xi, 3, 6, 7, 12, 13, 15, 16,
    21, 27, 34, 36, 37, 42, 49, 53, 64, 72,
    74, 77, 80, 83, 84, 85, 87, 94, 96, 99,
    100, 104, 105, 114
United States, vii, x, xi, 3, 6, 7, 12, 13,
    15, 16, 21, 27, 34, 36, 37, 42, 49, 53,
    64, 72, 74, 77, 80, 83, 84, 85, 87, 94,
    96, 99, 100, 104, 105, 114
universe, 111
updating, 120
urban, xi, 7, 8, 10, 14, 18, 19, 20, 22, 29,
    31, 40, 56, 99, 101
urban areas, 7, 14, 18, 19, 20, 31, 56, 101
USA, ix, 4, 51
utilization, viii, 3, 26, 63, 81

V

valuation, 10
variations, 88
vehicles, 7, 9, 18, 21, 23, 24, 28, 29, 31,
    60, 64, 88
vibration, 29, 31
vision, 55

volatile organic compounds, 52, 55
vulnerability, 39, 92

W

wages, 17
waiver, x, 5
war, 8, 32, 90
Washington, 86, 90, 94, 95, 96, 119
waste, 31
water, vii, x, 5, 6, 7, 8, 10, 11, 12, 13, 14, 15, 17, 20, 21, 22, 23, 24, 25, 27, 29, 30, 31, 32, 38, 39, 40, 41, 44, 52, 53, 54, 57, 60, 61, 64, 65, 66, 67, 69, 70, 72, 73, 74, 77, 78, 79, 84, 85, 89, 92, 93, 94, 96, 104, 106, 107, 109, 113, 118
water quality, 24
water resources, 32

waterborne, vii, x, xi, 5, 6, 8, 12, 41, 45, 64, 66, 71, 72, 78, 79, 81, 91, 100, 101, 104, 113, 114, 118
waterways, vii, x, xi, 3, 6, 12, 15, 21, 27, 31, 34, 40, 41, 44, 48, 49, 52, 57, 66, 77, 78, 81, 86, 99, 100, 101, 106, 117, 118
wear, viii, 3, 22, 55, 56, 57
web, 93, 97
web sites, 93
wetlands, 31, 32
White House, 85, 89
wholesale, 57
workers, 15, 16, 17, 37, 41, 53
workforce, 65
World War I, 111

Y

yield, 27, 49, 62